MASTER CLASS

AT JOHNSON & WALES

Cuisinart
SAVOR THE GOOD LIFE

weber

Cascade

MASTER CLASS

AT JOHNSON & WALES

Recipes from the Public Television Series

Produced by Marjorie Poore Productions

Photography by Alec Fatalevich

✈ TABLE OF CONTENTS

INTRODUCTION

Little did we know when we launched "Master Class at Johnson & Wales" on public television in 2002, that the program would enjoy a highly-successful first-run on PBS stations around the nation, today reaching more than 90 percent of all U.S. households. For close to three decades, Johnson & Wales University has set the highest standards in culinary education for students from around the world. Through "Master Class" and its companion cookbook, the techniques and cuisines that reflect the art and science of the culinary profession are now accessible to the home cook as well as the seasoned chef.

In the second season of "Master Class" and this accompanying cookbook, focus is on the techniques—brining, braising, poaching, knife skills among them—that are fundamental to developing the culinary expertise at the heart of all great cooking. Viewers get a behind-the-scenes look at the kitchens and hands-on training that surround students of culinary arts, baking and pastry arts, and culinary nutrition at the world's largest food service educator. Our goal is to provide the home cook with easy-to-prepare, nutritious, yet flavor-filled meals using a variety of preparation methods presented to expand the capabilities of novice and veteran alike.

Recipes are organized by courses—from healthful starters and delectable sides to exotic entrées and decadent desserts. While heavily influenced by international trends and traditional favorites, the recipes presented are infused with nutritional value. Whether a vegetarian specialty like Spicy Lentil Burger, a tried and true All American Baked Macaroni and Cheese, a regional sensation like Cajun Brined Smoked Turkey or a timeless international comfort food like Wiener Schnitzel, adaptations and ingredients make for not only healthy, but taste-tempting cuisine.

In preparing for this second season of "Master Class," we turned to yet another tier of experts with ties to Johnson & Wales. Recipes reflect the creativity of J&W's own chef instructors, and the mastery of such visiting guest chefs as Jasper White, Rose Levy Beranbaum and Lidia Bastianich. Among our contributors are alumni like Daniel Orr '85, executive chef at New York's famed Guastavino's and Loren Falsone '90, named among *Food & Wine* magazine's 10 Best New Chefs for 2000. Here we have blended the practical with the educational and served up a guide to replicating the extraordinary fare for which our contributors are famous.

Filming for the show was done at our campuses in North Miami, Florida and Providence, Rhode Island. Viewers again get a stove-side vantage point for viewing the hands-on learning for which our institution has world renown. In our first series, emphasis was on international cuisines adapted for the fast-paced tempo of 21st-century life. Now we bring you step-by-step demonstrations of the myriad of methods evolved over centuries for preparing food, preserving nutrients, instilling flavor and capturing the essences of ingredients. Within these pages you will find concise, easy-to-follow recipes that will allow you to recreate dishes featured in our series. It is our hope that by imparting knowledge of the most basic and time-honed techniques, and the recipes for these exceptional concoctions, we are freeing both our students and our viewers to explore the unending variations that the combination of imagination and skill can bring to the preparation of every meal. As they say in the vernacular, *bon appetit!*

✦ ACKNOWLEDGMENTS

The College of Culinary Arts at Johnson & Wales - America's Career University® - offers two- and four-year degree programs in culinary arts, and baking and pastry arts. Students also may continue their studies toward a bachelor of science degree in culinary nutrition, foodservice entrepreneurship, foodservice management and food marketing. More than 5,600 students are enrolled in culinary arts programs offered at the University's campuses in Providence, R.I., Charleston, S.C., Norfolk, Va., North Miami, Fla., and Denver, Colo., with plans to open a new campus in Charlotte, N.C. in 2004. For more information about Johnson & Wales University, visit www.jwu.edu

No project of this kind is possible without the dedication and efforts of a huge team of professionals and the support of a generous group of sponsors. We would like to thank the companies and individuals responsible for bringing this project to fruition, and their contributions to the success of the program. Through them, the viewing public has been exposed to the brand of culinary education for which Johnson & Wales University is known around the globe.

At the top of our list is Cuisinart, the company we are proud to call our inaugural sponsor. From the folks who brought the food processor from France to the masses and revolutionized the kitchen appliance industry, have come not only equipment and products, but people like Lee Rizzuto and Mary Rodgers. Their energy and commitment have made our efforts a pleasure, and theirs an invaluable asset to production.

Our chefs and students are especially grateful for the high-quality grilling equipment supplied by Weber-Stephen Products Company. In an industry driven by a zealous group of amateur chefs, Weber has managed to lead the country in manufacturing the best-line of grilling tools available to home cooks. Special thanks to Michael Kempster Sr. for backing our series with such unflagging enthusiasm.

We have Marjorie Poore Productions and the team of Marjorie Poore, director, Alec Fatalevich, executive producer and Deanna Sison, associate producer to thank for spotlighting the best of what makes culinary education at Johnson & Wales a student-focused, creative adventure. Their insight and dedication, combined with their technical expertise provided a dynamic setting for our students and chefs.

On our home front, we offer our gratitude to Johnson & Wales University President John Yena; Providence Campus President John Bowen '77 and Florida Campus President Donald McGregor for providing both the environment and support necessary to undertake this endeavor. We extend special kudos and heartfelt thanks to the entire team at our Florida Campus: Chef Rene Arnet, Don Cannon, Joseph Conlon '02, Michael Graziotti, Ron Hughes, Chef Michael Lyle '03, Chef Michael Moskwa, Shawn Ray '97, Rosibel Scafidi, Zoraya Suarez and Chef Chris Wagner. Their counterparts and cohorts from the Providence Campus deserve equal praise. Judi Johnson, Piya Sarawgi '94, '02 MBA, Chef Steven Shipley '85 and Miriam Weinstein covered many miles and coordinated a multitude of details behind the scenes.

And when it comes to more apparent behind-the-scenes efforts, we have Brett Bailey to thank for making us all look good in front of the cameras and on the pages of this cookbook, and Ken DellaPenta for his help organizing the wealth of information enclosed in these covers.

We are especially grateful to our distinguished guest chefs. For professionals of their caliber and fame to take time from their careers to enrich us with their contributions, underscores their commitment to education and to making their art form accessible to the students at their sides and the viewing public. That they participate on behalf of Johnson & Wales is an honor we hold in the highest regard.

And to the students and chefs who are the true measure of what makes culinary education at Johnson & Wales a masterful pursuit in any class, our admiration and appreciation. You serve as our guides in an ever-evolving and exciting frontier.

Karl Guggenmos '93, '02 MBA
Dean of the College of Culinary Arts
Johnson & Wales University

Chef Instructors

Christian Finck '96
Karl Guggenmos '93, '02 MBA
Diane Madsen '87, '99 MAT
Michael Moskwa
Harry Peemoeller
Peter Reinhart
Steve Shipley '85
Frank Terranova '94
Chris Wagner

Distinguished Guest Chefs

Lidia Bastianich
Rose Levy Beranbaum
David Burke
Loren Falsone '90
Michael Lomonaco
Daniel Orr '85
Steve Schimoler
Jud Simpson
Jasper White

Florida Campus Students

Tiffany Acero
Barbara Antoniou
Charalambous Argyro
Alexis Braguta
Adrianne Calvo
Suzanne Chin
Megan Connetti
Merielle Cruz
Cameron Hollerman
Matthew Holmes
Eric Dougherty
Sheigh Jackson
George Kokkinos
Karen Ley
Frank B. Lowry III
Adriel Martinetti

Lorna Martinez
Bobby Moody
Jean C. Pérez Pillot
Christopher Valentine
Kyle Williams
Brian Willoughby

Providence Campus Students

Abhishek Abbi
Avi Altman
Gina Ancelli
Crystal Brennan
Nathaniel Brethold
Adam Gibby
Jane Guild
Gregory Javonillo
Jennifer Kane
Kim McMahon
Justin Perkins
Alexander Ryser
Tavis Schafer
Eric Stein
Allison Steven
Tracy Wilczek

STARTERS, SIDES AND SAUCES

✢ BEAN, AVOCADO AND TOMATO SALAD

This cool, refreshing salad is simple to prepare and will round out your brunch menu perfectly. If unable to locate lollo rossa lettuce, use just the center sections of the nicest heads of red leaf lettuce that you can find.

Chili Vinaigrette:

2 tablespoons red wine vinegar

$^1/_2$ teaspoon granulated sugar

1 tablespoon chopped fresh parsley

1 teaspoon chili powder

1 teaspoon coriander seeds, lightly toasted,
  and cracked

4 tablespoons olive oil

Bean, Avocado and Tomato Salad:

2 cups fresh green beans, ends trimmed, blanched
  in boiling salted water

2 whole ripe avocados

1 tablespoon fresh-squeezed lemon juice

$^1/_2$ pound lollo rossa lettuce, root ends removed,
  washed, and spun dry

8 cherry tomatoes, washed, and cut in half widthwise

1 medium red onion (about 4 ounces), root end removed,
  peeled, cut in half lengthwise, and sliced thin

To make the chili vinaigrette:

Combine vinegar and sugar in a small noncorrosive bowl. Stir with a wire whisk to dissolve the sugar. Add parsley, chili powder, and coriander and stir to combine. Slowly drizzle olive oil into the bowl while whisking vigorously. Continue to whisk the vinaigrette for 1 minute after oil has been added. Set aside.

To make the salad:

Bring $1^1/_2$ quarts of lightly salted water to a boil in a large saucepot over high heat. Add green beans and blanch until just tender—about $2^1/_2$ minutes. Immediately transfer to an ice water bath. Drain the water and set aside.

Using a sharp knife, cut avocados in half lengthwise around the pit. Using a twisting motion, split in half. Hold the side of the avocado that still has the pit in one hand and a sharp knife in the other. Firmly, but carefully, tap the knife handle with the heel of your hand so the blade sticks in the pit. Simply twist the knife while holding the avocado in place and the pit will pop right out. Discard the pit and repeat with the second avocado. Peel the avocado using your fingers or a soup spoon. Slice into thin strips and immediately sprinkle with lemon juice to keep from oxidizing and turning brown.

To serve the salad:

Line 4 salad bowls with equal amounts of the lollo rossa lettuce. Artfully arrange the sliced avocados, onions, and split cherry tomatoes on the salad greens leaving a space in the center. Place green beans in the center. Lightly whisk the dressing and drizzle an equal amount over each of the salads and serve.

✹ CHEF'S NOTE: Don't cover the saucepot while blanching the beans, it causes them to discolor.

4 SERVINGS

GRILLED SUMMER VEGETABLES WITH FRESH BASIL AND BALSAMIC VINEGAR

When grilling side dishes, it is advisable to grill your vegetables before the meat, and place them on indirect heat until you're ready to serve them.

1 medium green bell pepper, washed, stem removed, seeded, pith removed, and cut into quarters lengthwise

1 medium red bell pepper, washed, stem removed, seeded, pith removed, and cut into quarters lengthwise

1 medium orange bell pepper, washed, stem removed, seeded, pith removed and cut into quarters lengthwise

4 Japanese eggplants, washed, stem end removed, and cut in half lengthwise

1 medium red onion, peeled, and cut into 8 wedges, lengthwise with root ends attached

4 scallions, washed and ends trimmed

4 large portobello mushrooms, about 4–5 inches in diameter, stems and black gills removed

2 medium zucchini (about 1 pound), washed, ends removed, cut in quarters lengthwise

2 medium yellow squash (about 1 pound), washed, ends removed, cut in quarters lengthwise

4 medium plum tomatoes (about 12 ounces), washed, stem ends removed, and cut in half lengthwise

1 pound asparagus, washed, woody stems trimmed off, ends peeled, blanched in boiling salted water, and shocked in ice water

1/2 cup olive oil

1/4 cup fresh basil leaves, cut into thin strips

2 tablespoons balsamic vinegar

To grill the vegetables:
Preheat the grill to medium-high.

Lightly brush all of the vegetables with some of the olive oil, and season with salt and pepper. Grill the vegetables for 5 minutes on each side until tender. Remove the vegetables from the grill and artfully arrange them on a serving platter. Sprinkle strips of basil and the balsamic vinegar over the top to garnish, and serve immediately.

CHEF'S NOTE: The vegetables may be grilled on a vegetable rack, available at most hardware or kitchen supply stores. For the best result, blanch the heartier green vegetables before grilling.

4 SERVINGS

→ GRILLED SHRIMP WITH CRACKED BULGHUR WHEAT SALAD

Healthy, low-fat, easy and above all, tasty! Just a few reasons why this salad is a must try. Simmer the bulghur wheat in a well-seasoned chicken stock to give it an even richer flavor.

Bulghur Wheat Salad:

2 cups bulghur wheat

5 cups cold water

1 small red onion, root end removed (about 4 ounces), peeled and thinly sliced

2 cloves garlic, root end removed, peeled and crushed

1 large tomato (about 8 ounces), cored, scored, blanched, skin and seeds removed, and diced into ¹/₂-inch pieces

1 head broccoli, washed, cut into small flowerettes, blanched in lightly salted boiling water; then shocked in ice water

¹/₄ cup dried cranberries

¹/₄ cup pine nuts, toasted

¹/₂ cup chopped parsley

1 tablespoon fresh-squeezed lemon juice

¹/₄ cup extra virgin olive oil

¹/₂ teaspoon ground cinnamon

¹/₂ teaspoon ground cumin

Salt and pepper

1 scallion, washed, ends trimmed, and thinly sliced

Shrimp:

1 tablespoon olive oil

2 tablespoons hoisin sauce

1 tablespoon water

16 U-12 tiger shrimp

Salt and pepper

4 bamboo skewers

To make the bulghur wheat salad:

Cover the bulghur wheat with 5 cups cold water. Place in the refrigerator and allow the wheat to absorb the water for 2 hours or overnight. Drain and rinse the wheat under cold running water. Use your hands to squeeze as much water from the wheat as possible. Place the wheat in a large bowl and add the remaining ingredients for the salad. Mix with a spoon until well combined. Cover with plastic wrap and refrigerate for 1 hour.

To grill the shrimp:

Combine the olive oil, hoisin sauce, and water in a medium bowl, and mix with a spoon to combine. Add the shrimp and toss to coat. Allow the shrimp to marinate for 30 minutes.

Soak 4 wooden skewers in water for at least 1 hour before skewering and grilling to prevent them from burning on the grill. You may use metal skewers instead.

Preheat a grill pan or your outdoor grill to medium heat.

Remove the shrimp from the marinade and arrange them on the work surface so that each 4-shrimp portion may be secured with 2 skewers, one through the head section and one through the tail section. Season the shrimp with salt and pepper.

Grill the shrimp for about 1¹/₂ to 2 minutes on each side until tender. Remove and discard the wooden skewers from each portion of shrimp. Place the shrimp on the bulghur wheat salad and serve immediately.

☆ CHEF'S NOTE: Shrimp are packed and sold by the average number of shrimp in a pound. U-12 refers to fewer than 12 per pound. If you are unable to find U-12 shrimp 16/20 shrimp will work quite nicely. Use 6 to 8 per skewer if you use smaller shrimp.

4 SERVINGS

⇢ GRILLED MARINATED SHRIMP AND CITRUS SALAD

Tangy fruit and flavorful shrimp combine to create a sweet yet spicy summer salad. Serve this as a prelude to a meal, or as a healthy entrée.

Marinade:

2 tablespoons fresh-squeezed lemon juice

1 tablespoon olive oil

Salt and black pepper

2 pounds 16/20 count tiger shrimp, peel removed, and de-veined

Citrus Salad:

2 large grapefruit, peel removed, sectioned, and juices reserved

2 large navel oranges, peel removed, sectioned, and juices reserved

$^1/_4$ cup thinly-sliced red onion

$^1/_4$ cup small-diced celery

$^1/_2$ medium red bell pepper (about 3 ounces), thinly sliced

$^1/_2$ cup olive oil

2 tablespoons apple cider vinegar

1 teaspoon dry mustard

1 tablespoon minced onion

1 teaspoon granulated sugar

Salt and black pepper

1 large head Romaine lettuce (about 1$^1/_2$ pounds)

To make the marinade:

Place the shrimp into a medium, noncorrosive bowl. Add lemon juice and olive oil, and stir to combine. Season with salt and pepper; cover with plastic wrap and refrigerate for 1 hour.

To make the citrus salad:

Combine grapefruit sections, orange sections, red onion, celery, and red pepper in a medium bowl and set aside.

In another medium bowl, combine the reserved citrus juices, olive oil, vinegar, dry mustard, minced onion, and sugar. Season with salt and pepper and whisk vigorously to combine. Add $^1/_4$-cup of the dressing to the citrus salad and stir to combine. Set the salad and the remaining dressing aside at room temperature until needed.

Remove and discard any unsightly outer leaves from the head of romaine. One by one break the leaves off from the root of the head of lettuce. Reserve 8 of the nicest inner leaves for presentation. Cut the remaining leaves widthwise into 1-inch-thick strips. Place 2 whole leaves onto each of the 4 plates. Arrange an equal amount of the cut greens onto the center of each plate topped with an equal portion of the citrus salad. Dress the greens with the remaining vinaigrette and set aside.

To grill the shrimp:

Preheat the grill to medium heat.

Soak 8 wooden skewers in water for at least 1 hour before skewering and grilling to prevent them from burning on the grill. You could use metal skewers instead of the wooden or bamboo varieties.

Remove the shrimp from the marinade and lay them out on a clean, sanitized work surface in 4 equal piles (There should be about 9 shrimp per pile.) Arrange the shrimp on the work surface so each 9-shrimp portion may be secured with 2

skewers, one through the head section and one through the tail section. Season the shrimp with salt and pepper.

Grill the shrimp for about 1½ to 2 minutes on each side until tender. Remove and discard the wooden skewers from the shrimp. Place the shrimp around the citrus salad on the plate, and serve immediately.

✳ **CHEF'S NOTE:** Keep the grill covered when cooking to impart a good smoky flavor and even cooking temperature, but be aware that the shrimp will cook very quickly. Remove all the white "pith" from the citrus fruit when peeling to avoid any bitter flavor to the citrus salad.

4 SERVINGS

→ RED LENTIL SALAD WITH SPINACH AND GOLDEN RAISINS

With distinct Eastern spices and ingredients, this salad is exotic, but easy to prepare and serve. If you are unable to locate red lentils, you could make this salad with brown, or French green lentils.

Red Lentils and Salad:

1 pound dried lentils, picked through, washed, and drained

1 cup golden raisins

$1/3$ cup capers, rinsed

1 large red onion (about 8 ounces), root end removed, peeled and diced into $1/4$-inch pieces

1 cup flat leaf spinach (about 2 ounces), washed, spun dry, and cut into $1/4$-inch strips

1 medium zucchini (about 8 ounces washed), ends removed, cut into long thin strips

1 medium yellow squash (about 8 ounces), ends removed, washed and cut into long thin strips

2 Belgian endive (about 12 ounces), root end trimmed, peddles removed, washed, and patted dry

Spiced Vinaigrette:

$1/2$ cup white wine vinegar

2 tablespoons granulated sugar

2 teaspoons salt

2 teaspoons black pepper

1 teaspoon ground cumin

1 teaspoon dry mustard

$1/2$ teaspoon turmeric

$1/2$ teaspoon ground mace

$1/4$ teaspoon cayenne pepper

$3/4$ cup olive oil

To make the lentils and salad:

Place lentils in a medium saucepan and cover with 1 quart of cold water. Bring to a simmer over medium high heat. Continue to simmer for 30 minutes until tender, but not soggy or falling apart. Drain lentils in a colander and season with salt and pepper. Transfer steaming lentils to a baking sheet with sides and refrigerate until cold. Make the vinaigrette while the lentils chill.

To make the vinaigrette:

Combine all the ingredients, with the exception of the olive oil, in a medium bowl. Stir with a wire whisk to combine. Slowly drizzle olive oil into the bowl of spices and vinegar while whisking vigorously. Continue to whisk the vinaigrette for 1 minute after the oil has been added.

Once the lentils are cold, transfer them to a medium bowl. Add the vinaigrette and mix to combine. Cover the bowl with plastic wrap and refrigerate overnight.

Two hours before serving, add the raisins, capers, and red onion. Stir to incorporate. Rewrap and return to the refrigerator until ready to serve.

To serve the lentil salad:

Bring 1 quart of salted water to a boil over high heat. Blanch the zucchini and yellow squash for 15 seconds in the boiling water until just tender. Immediately transfer them to an ice water bath. Drain the water from the blanched zucchini and yellow squash, and pat them dry with absorbent towels.

Place the Belgian endive spears evenly around the outer edge of each of 4 plates. Form a ring or a nest of the zucchini and yellow squash in the center of the plate covering just the cut ends of the endive spears. Evenly portion the red lentil salad in the center of the vegetable nests and serve.

✳ **CHEF'S NOTE:** Place a damp towel under the bowl while you whisk your dressing. This keeps the bowl steady so you can drizzle the oil and whisk at the same time.

4 SERVINGS

✛ PURÉE OF TUSCAN BEAN SOUP

This soup can be prepared the day before and reheated just in time for your guests to enjoy. Serve with some crusty bread and a simple salad. You may also make this soup with navy beans or great northern beans.

3 strips bacon, chopped fine

1 small onion (about 4 ounces), root end removed, peeled and diced into ¹/₄-inch pieces

1 medium carrot (about 3 ounces), ends removed, peeled and diced into ¹/₄-inch pieces

1 large stalk celery, washed and diced into ¹/₄-inch pieces

6 cloves garlic, peeled, root ends removed, and mashed into a puree

Salt and pepper

1¹/₂ quarts chicken stock

2 medium ham hocks (about 1 pound)

1 pound dried white cannellini beans, picked through, washed, and soaked in cold water in the refrigerator overnight, then drained and rinsed

2 large tomatoes (about 1 pound) peeled, seeds removed, and chopped into ¹/₄-inch pieces

2 teaspoons chopped fresh marjoram

2 cups fresh croutons

To make the soup:

Heat a medium stock pot over medium high heat. When hot, add bacon and cook, stirring frequently for 3 minutes, until slightly golden. Add diced onion, carrot, and celery, season with salt and pepper, and sauté vegetables until onions become translucent—about 4 minutes. Add garlic paste and sauté for an additional minute. Add stock, beans, and ham hocks and bring to a boil. Reduce the heat and simmer until the beans are tender about 1¹/₂ hours.

Remove the ham hock from the soup. Discard the skin and bones. Using a sharp knife dice the meat into ¹/₄-inch pieces and set aside.

Transfer half of the soup to a food processor fitted with a metal blade and purée until smooth. Pour the purée back into the stock pot with the original soup, and stir to combine. Add tomatoes and diced ham. Adjust the seasoning with salt and pepper. Add marjoram and stir to incorporate. Serve in warm bowls with a few fresh croutons. If you don't have a food processor, use an immersion blender or a conventional blender.

✺ **CHEF'S NOTE:** Pick through the beans and remove dirt or rocks that are often found in dried beans. Do not add salt to the water in which they are soaking as it will cause the shell of the bean to harden. Also, it is important to soak the beans in the refrigerator so they don't spoil. Cover the beans with a bit more than twice the amount of water by volume; they will absorb a lot over the course of a few hours.

10 SERVINGS

✧ PURÉE OF SPLIT PEA SOUP

Soup is a traditional, hearty winter dish. For a colorful change, you may substitute golden split peas or coral split peas instead of the green variety when making this soup.

1 tablespoon vegetable oil

4 ounces smoked bacon, diced into $^1/_4$-inch pieces

1 small onion (about 4 ounces), root end removed, peeled and diced into $^1/_4$-inch pieces

1 medium carrot (about 3 ounces), ends removed, peeled and diced into $^1/_4$-inch pieces

1 large stalk celery, washed and diced into $^1/_4$-inch pieces

Salt and white pepper

4 cloves garlic, root end removed, peeled and crushed

2 quarts vegetable stock

1 pound split peas, picked through, washed, and soaked in cold water in the refrigerator overnight, then drained and rinsed

2 medium ham hocks (about 1 pound)

2 cups fresh croutons

To make the soup:

Heat oil in a medium stock pot over medium high heat. When hot, add bacon and cook stirring frequently for 3 minutes, until slightly golden. Add diced onion, carrot, and celery, season with salt and white pepper, and sauté vegetables until onions become translucent—about 4 minutes. Add garlic cloves and sauté for an additional minute. Add stock, peas, and ham hocks. Bring to a boil. Reduce the heat and simmer until the peas are tender— about 1$^1/_2$ hours.

Remove the ham hock from the soup. Discard the skin and the bones. Using a sharp knife, dice the meat into $^1/_4$-inch pieces and set aside.

Transfer $^1/_2$ the soup to a food processor fitted with a metal blade and purée until smooth. Pour the purée back into the stockpot with the original soup, and stir to combine. Add diced ham. Adjust the seasoning with salt and pepper. Serve in warm bowls with a few fresh croutons. If you don't have a food processor, use an immersion blender or a conventional blender.

✳ CHEF'S NOTE: To make croutons, simply dice a couple of slices of day-old bread. Drizzle a few tablespoons of oil over them. Toss with salt and pepper and toast in a preheated 325° oven until golden brown and crunchy—about 6 minutes.

10 SERVINGS

⊹ GRILLED SOUTHEAST ASIAN SHRIMP WITH UDON NOODLES IN MISO BROTH

This soup is a complete meal in itself. Udon noodles are a wheat product, similar to pasta and the miso broth has a distinctive flavor to it. All of the ingredients in the broth are available at Asian markets and many large supermarkets.

Asian Marinade:

12 large (U-12) fresh shrimp, peeled and de-veined

4 sugar cane skewers, each about 4 inches long

1/4 cup peanut oil

3 tablespoon rice wine vinegar

1 tablespoon light soy sauce

1 tablespoon honey

1 tablespoon molasses

1 tablespoon chopped fresh garlic

1 tablespoon minced fresh ginger

1 whole scallion, washed, ends trimmed and chopped

1 tablespoon garlic chili paste

1/2 teaspoon kosher salt

1/4 teaspoon fresh ground black pepper

Udon Noodles and Miso Broth:

4 cups water

1 piece dried kelp (kombu)

1 tablespoon bonito flakes

4 tablespoons miso paste

1/4 cup sliced green scallions

2 teaspoons soy sauce

2 teaspoons garlic chili paste

8 ounces udon noodles, cooked

To make the Asian marinade:
Skewer 3 shrimp on each of the sugar cane skewers. Place the skewered shrimp in a casserole dish and set aside while preparing the marinade.

Combine the remaining ingredients for the marinade in a medium bowl and stir with a wire whisk until thoroughly combined. Pour this marinade over the skewered shrimp, cover with plastic wrap, and refrigerate for 1 hour.

To make the miso broth:
Just before you cook the shrimp, heat the water, kelp, and bonito flakes in a medium saucepan over medium-high heat. Bring to a simmer and cook for 4 minutes. Strain the kelp and the flakes from the broth and discard. Return the broth to the heat and bring back to a simmer. Add the remaining ingredients for the broth and stir to combine. Reduce the heat to low while grilling the shrimp.

To grill the shrimp:
Preheat a grill pan or grill to medium heat. When hot, grill the shrimp skewers for 4 minutes on each side. While the shrimp are grilling, ladle 1 cup of the miso broth into each of 4 warm entrée bowls. Place an equal-sized portion of udon noodles in the center and top with a grilled shrimp skewer.

✳ CHEF'S NOTE: It may be difficult for you to locate sugar cane for the skewers. Bamboo skewers work well, but will not impart any sugar flavor to the shrimp. Soak the bamboo skewers in water for at least 1 hour prior to grilling to prevent them from burning.

4 SERVINGS

⊹ GRILLED VEGETARIAN PIZZA

Get versatile and serve this in small wedges as an appetizer. Or, get innovative and top your pizzas with your favorite vegetables - diced peppers, blanched asparagus, fresh-chopped herbs, sautéed wild mushrooms, specialty olives, and more.

Pizza Dough:

1 tablespoon cake yeast

1/2 cup warm water

1/4 cup milk

2 1/4 cups all-purpose flour

1/4 teaspoon salt

1/4 teaspoon olive oil

Vegetarian Pizzas:

1/4 cup extra virgin olive oil

1 teaspoon minced fresh garlic

1 28-ounce can whole peeled Italian plum tomatoes, drained and hand crushed

1 teaspoon kosher salt

1/2 teaspoon fresh ground black pepper

1 teaspoon dried oregano

1 tablespoon dried basil

1 cup chopped scallions

1/4 cup fresh basil, cut into thin strips

1 cup shredded cheese (preferably a mix of fresh mozzarella and Fontina)

To make the pizza dough:

Combine yeast and water in a small bowl and stir with a small spoon until the yeast has dissolved completely—about 2 minutes. Place the flour in a food processor fitted with a dough blade. Add salt to the yeast and water mixture. Operate the mixer on pulse for 30 seconds to combine, then switch to full speed and allow the dough to mix until it forms a solid mass—about 1 minute. Transfer the dough to a clean, dry work surface. Use your hands to knead the dough for 3 minutes. Lightly coat the inside of a medium bowl with olive oil. Place the dough in the prepared bowl. Cover with a towel and place in a warm place to rise until doubled in size—about 1 hour.

Use your hands to punch the dough down to its original size. Cover the bowl and allow the dough to rise once again until it is double in size—about 1 hour.

To grill the pizzas:

Heat 1 tablespoon of oil in a medium saucepan over medium heat. When hot, add garlic and sauté for 15 seconds, being careful not to brown. Add tomatoes and stir to incorporate. Season with salt and pepper; then add the dried herbs. Mix to combine. Allow the sauce to simmer on low heat for 20 minutes until slightly thickened. Transfer sauce to an ice bath and stir with a rubber spatula until cold. Refrigerate until needed.

Preheat half of the grill to medium, leaving the other side cool.

Cut dough into 4 equal pieces and lightly coat with the remaining olive oil. Set aside in a shallow dish. Place one of the dough balls on a clean, dry work surface. Use your hands to press the dough out into circular shapes, starting in the center and working your way out to the edges until thin. Set aside while pressing out the other three balls. One at a time, gently stretch each piece of dough to

make thin again and place on the grill until the edges begin to puff up a little bit—about 3 minutes. The underside of the dough should be lightly crisp. Quickly turn the dough over onto the cool side of the grill. Immediately spread tomato sauce over the grilled surface of the bread. Sprinkle the sauced pizza with vegetable toppings of your choice, being sure not to overload the small pizzas. Top with the grated cheeses, then sprinkle generously with chopped scallions and sliced basil. Close the grill cover and cook pizza on indirect heat for another 2–3 minutes or until cheese is fully melted. Remove pizza from grill, hold warm, and follow

these steps to finish the 3 remaining pizzas. Cut the pizzas into wedges and serve immediately.

✳ **CHEF'S NOTE:** Use cake-style yeast instead of dry active yeast. If using dry active yeast, use $1\frac{1}{2}$ tablespoons instead of 1 tablespoon. A great place to proof dough (raise it) is in a gas oven with ONLY the pilot light on.

4 SERVINGS

✦ MUSHROOM TARTE TATIN

Taken from Chef Schimoler's cookbook *The Mist Grill: Rustic Cooking from Vermont*, this recipe, initially designed as a vegetarian menu item, quickly evolved to be a favorite of customers for its rich and bold flavors.

Parmesan Anglaise:

1 cup heavy cream
1/2 cup grated Parmesan cheese
1 large egg yolk
Salt and pepper

Mushroom Tarte Tatin

One sheet frozen puff pastry dough
1 tablespoon unsalted butter
1 medium shallot, peeled, root end removed and minced
1 teaspoon minced garlic
1/2 cup sliced shiitake caps
1 large portobello mushroom cap (about 6 ounces), gills removed and sliced thin
1 small clump oyster mushrooms, torn into long pieces
1/2 cup sliced chanterelle mushrooms
Salt and pepper
1 teaspoon chopped fresh rosemary
1 1/2 teaspoons truffle oil
1 teaspoon cracked black pepper
1 2-inch rosemary sprig

To make the Parmesan anglaise:

Heat the cream in a medium saucepan over medium-high heat. Bring to a boil; then reduce and simmer until the cream has reduced by almost half — about 14 minutes. Remove from the heat and set aside at room temperature to cool for 10 minutes. Add egg yolk and cheese and whisk vigorously to combine. Place the sauce back onto the range over low heat, and stir until it begins to simmer again. Adjust the seasoning with salt and pepper. Remove from heat and keep warm.

To bake the tarte tartin:

Preheat the oven to 350°.
Using an 8-inch sauté pan as a template; cut a circle out of the pastry sheet to match the dimension of your sauté pan, and set aside.

Heat butter in the sauté pan over medium-high heat. When hot, add the shallots and garlic, and stir constantly for about 30 seconds. Add mushrooms and herbs, and stir occasionally for 2 minutes, until soft. Remove from the range. Place the pastry disc on top of the mushroom mix, sealing the pan. Bake on the center rack of the preheated oven for approximately 8 minutes or until the pastry is ballooned and rich golden brown.

Remove from the oven and turn the tart out onto a plate, so the pastry crust is on the bottom and the mushrooms are facing up. Immediately return the pan to the stovetop, pour about a 1/2 cup of the Parmesan anglaise into the pan and bring to a boil—about 1 minute. Drizzle sauce around the perimeter of the plate and tart. Drizzle truffle oil on the tart and in the anglaise. Garnish with cracked pepper and rosemary sprig. Serve immediately.

✴ **CHEF'S NOTE:** The Parmesan anglaise will keep in the refrigerator for 2 – 3 days. Simply simmer before serving.

2 SERVINGS

✧ STUFFED PORTOBELLO MUSHROOMS

You could very easily convert this dish into a vegetarian entrée by simply eliminating the cooked ham from the recipe. If wild rice is not available or just not to your taste, feel free to substitute brown rice.

4 large portobello mushrooms, about 4–5 inches in
    diameter, stems and black gills removed, if desired
$^1/_4$ cup balsamic vinegar
$^1/_4$ cup olive oil
2 cups cooked wild rice
8 ounces smoked cooked ham, diced into $^1/_4$-inch pieces
8 ounces roasted red pepper, diced into $^1/_4$-inch pieces
1 tablespoon fresh chopped thyme
Salt and pepper
8 ounces flat leaf spinach, washed and spun dry

To make the stuffed mushrooms:
Place a mushroom cap top side down, in the center of each of 4 pieces of non-stick aluminum foil. Combine 2 tablespoons of vinegar and 2 tablespoons of oil in a small bowl with a spoon, then drizzle it over each of the four caps.

Combine wild rice, ham, peppers, and thyme in a medium bowl. Drizzle the rice and vegetable mixture with 1 tablespoon each vinegar and olive oil. Season with salt and pepper, and mix until well combined. Top the caps with equal amounts of rice and vegetable mixture, and press down gently to make a mound. Pull up the sides of the foil, and bring them together at the top. Triple fold the foil ends creating a tube shape, leaving about 1 inch of

room between the foil fold and the food. Triple fold the sides of the tube, creating a sealed packet. Place the 4 packets on a baking sheet with sides and place in the oven to bake for 18 to 20 minutes.

Remove the tray from the oven. Use a pair of tongs to open the packets of stuffed mushrooms. Be careful, there will be a considerable amount of steam ready to escape the packets as soon as they are opened.

Drizzle the remaining tablespoon of oil and vinegar onto the spinach, and toss well to combine. Evenly divide the spinach between 4 plates. Place a stuffed portobello on top of each pile of spinach, and serve immediately.

✤ **CHEF'S NOTE:** The gills on the mushroom caps lend a strong woodsy flavor to the finished dish. If you do decide to remove the gills, the easiest way to do so is to use a teaspoon to gently scrape them off. If you are unable to find non-stick foil in your local grocery, use a heavy-duty aluminum foil instead. Be sure to spray the foil with non-stick cooking spray or lightly brush with vegetable oil.

4 SERVINGS

→ SPICY LENTIL BURGERS

A great recipe for vegetarians and non-vegetarians alike who are looking to add protein to their diet. Personalize your lentil burgers with your preferred toppings, or serve on the bread of your choice. You can use your favorite type of lentils for this recipe – be careful not to overcook brown or French green lentils.

1 pound dried lentils, picked through, washed, and drained

Salt and pepper

4 tablespoons olive oil

1 medium onion (about 4 ounces), peeled, core removed, and minced

2 medium carrots (about 5 ounces), ends removed, peeled and chopped fine

1 clove garlic, root end removed and minced

1/2 teaspoon ground cumin

1/2 teaspoon ground coriander

6 teaspoon chopped fresh parsley

18 medium shiitake mushrooms, stems removed

6 sesame seed burger buns

6 slices tomato

1/4 pound flat leaf spinach, washed and spun dry

To make the lentil burgers:

Place lentils in a medium saucepan, and cover with 1 quart of cold water. Bring to a simmer over medium heat. Continue to simmer for 30 minutes until tender, but not soggy. Drain lentils in a colander and season with salt and pepper. Transfer steaming lentils to a baking sheet with sides, and refrigerate until cold.

Heat 2 tablespoons of oil in a large sauté pan over medium-high heat. When hot, add onion and carrot, season with salt and pepper, and sauté until tender—about 3 minutes. Add garlic and continue to cook for 30 seconds. Add cumin, coriander, and parsley, and stir to combine. Add cooked lentils, and stir to combine. Cook the lentil and spiced vegetable mixture for 3 minutes, stirring frequently to keep the lentils from burning. Transfer this mixture to a baking sheet with sides, and place in the refrigerator to cool.

To grill the lentil burgers:

Heat the grill to medium high heat.

Remove cold lentil mixture from the refrigerator. Use your hands to mash the bean mixture until it is slightly sticky, and form 6 large burgers. Place them on a platter, and refrigerate until needed.

Drizzle the remaining oil over the shiitake caps. Season them with salt and pepper. Grill the mushrooms for 2 minutes on each side. Remove them from the grill and hold warm.

Season the burgers on each side with salt and pepper. Grill them for 3 to 4 minutes on each side.

Toast the buns on the grill until golden brown—about 1 minute on each side. Gently place a lentil burger on each toasted bun. Top the burger with grilled shiitakes, sliced tomatoes, and spinach leaves. Serve immediately with your favorite condiments.

✹ CHEF'S NOTE: The burgers are very fragile so handle them with care on the grill or in a large sauté pan.

6 SERVINGS

↝ ROASTED ROOT VEGETABLE CASSEROLE WITH CHÉVRE CHEESE AND CAESAR CRUMB TOPPING

This hearty vegetable casserole could be served as an accompaniment to the main meal, or could be the feature item on your menu. Get creative if you want and incorporate your favorite cheese and root vegetables.

Caesar crumb topping:

1 1/2 cups fresh bread cut into 1/4-inch pieces

1 teaspoon dried Italian seasoning

1/2 teaspoon granulated garlic

2 tablespoons grated Parmesan cheese

1 tablespoon fresh chopped parsley

2 tablespoons olive oil

Root vegetable casserole:

1 head fresh garlic, peeled and root end removed

3 medium carrots (about 10 ounces), ends removed, peeled and diced into 1/2-inch pieces

3 medium parsnips (about 8 ounces), ends removed, peeled and diced into 1/2-inch pieces

2 medium turnips (about 10 ounces), ends trimmed, peeled and cut into 1/2-inch pieces

2 medium beets (about 10 ounces), ends trimmed, peeled and cut into 1/2-inch pieces

6 small purple potatoes (about 12 ounces), cut into 1/2-inch pieces

2 1/2 tablespoons olive oil

Salt and pepper

1/2 cup crumbled chévre cheese

1/2 cup vegetable broth

To make the Caesar crumb topping:
Place all of the ingredients for the topping in a medium bowl. Toss to combine, and set aside until needed.

To roast the root vegetable casserole:
Preheat the oven to 400°.

Place garlic bulbs, diced vegetables, and potatoes in a large bowl. Add olive oil, season with salt and pepper, and toss until all the vegetables are coated with oil. Transfer the vegetables to 2 non-stick baking sheets with sides and place in the oven to roast until lightly golden brown and tender—about 18 minutes.

Remove the roasted vegetables from the oven and transfer them back to the large bowl. Add the chévre cheese and vegetable broth, and toss to combine. Transfer this mixture to a large casserole dish. Top evenly with the Caesar crumb topping and bake in the preheated oven until the bread cubes are lightly toasted—about 10 minutes. Remove from the oven and serve immediately.

✺ **CHEF'S NOTE:** Substitute goat or feta cheese if you are unable to find chévre cheese in your local grocery or specialty shop.

SERVES 6

✦ BAKED MACARONI AND CHEESE

Comfort food is back! Make time to enjoy this American tradition with your closest friends and family members. Add you own personal flair by using your favorite pasta shape.

1 quart whole milk

1 small onion (about 3 ounces), peeled, and studded with 12 cloves

3 tablespoons clarified butter

3 tablespoons all-purpose flour

Salt and pepper

Pinch of nutmeg

1 cup heavy cream, warm

8 ounces sharp cheddar cheese, grated

1 pound elbow macaroni, cooked, and lightly oiled

1 cup corn flakes, slightly crushed

To make the macaroni and cheese:

Preheat the oven to 350°.

Heat the milk in a large saucepan over medium heat. When hot, add the studded onion, and simmer for 10 minutes.

While the milk and onion are simmering, heat the clarified butter in a small saucepan over medium heat. When hot, add the flour and stir with a small spoon to combine. This is called a roux. Allow the roux to cook stirring frequently for 6 minutes. Remove from the heat and set aside.

Remove the studded onion from the pot and discard. Vigorously whisk the simmering milk while you add the roux. Bring the slightly thickened milk mixture to a boil; then reduce the heat to low, and allow it to simmer for 10 minutes. Season with salt, pepper, and nutmeg; then add the warm heavy cream, and stir to combine. Slowly add about 2/3 of the cheese to the thickened milk and cream mixture while constantly stirring with a wire whisk until smooth. Adjust the seasoning with salt and pepper.

Place the cooked pasta in a large bowl. Pour the hot cheese sauce over the top of the macaroni, and stir with a rubber spatula until the macaroni is totally coated with cheese sauce. Transfer to a large, lightly greased casserole dish. Top with the remaining 1/3 of the grated cheddar cheese; then sprinkle the top with the corn flakes. Bake in the preheated oven for 25 minutes until bubbly. Remove from the oven, and allow to cool at room temperature for 10 minutes before serving.

✳ **CHEF'S NOTE:** A sharp white or orange cheddar cheese works best. Other cheeses don't lend themselves to this dish quite like cheddar. If your "mac-n-cheese" gets a little dark in the oven while baking, loosely cover the top with aluminum foil.

8 SERVINGS

→ CREAMY POLENTA TIMBALE WITH SPINACH, ROASTED RED PEPPER, AND PARMIGIANO-REGGIANO CHEESE

This colorful dish can be prepared ahead of time, and you may use any kind of mold to create a dramatic presentation for your guests. Rely on your favorite tomato sauce or try the fantastic marinara sauce recipe on page 44.

4 cups water

1 teaspoon salt

1 cup polenta (not instant)

2 ounces unsalted butter (^{1}/$_2$ stick), cut into
  ^{1}/$_2$ ounce pieces

^{1}/$_4$ cup fresh grated Parmigiano-Reggiano cheese

^{1}/$_2$ pound flat leaf spinach, washed, cooked, and
  drained of excess water

2 medium red bell peppers, fire roasted, charred skin,
  stem, seeds, and pith removed

2 tablespoons chopped fresh parsley

1 cup tomato sauce, hot

4 crispy fried basil leaves

To make the polenta:

Combine water and salt in a medium saucepan. Bring to a boil over medium-high heat. Reduce the heat to a simmer, and slowly add the polenta while constantly stirring with a wooden spoon. Continue to stir polenta for about 5 minutes until slightly thickened. Reduce the heat once more so the polenta is barely bubbling, and cook for about 30 minutes, stirring frequently, until it becomes quite thick. Remove the polenta from the heat. Stir in the butter and the cheese.

To assemble the timbales:

Preheat the oven to 350°.

Alternately layer the polenta, spinach, and roasted peppers in 4 lightly oiled soup cups or coffee cups until full. Place these into the oven to bake until all the layers are hot—about 8 minutes. Remove the cups from the oven. Portion 2 ounces of the hot tomato sauce into the center of each plate. Unmold the timbales onto a flat work surface. Use a spatula to place a timbale in the center of each plate. Garnish with a sprinkle of chopped parsley and a fried basil leaf. Serve immediately.

✳ **CHEF'S NOTE:** To fry the basil, simply heat ^{1}/$_2$-cup of vegetable oil in a small saucepan over medium heat until it reaches a temperature of 350°. Fry the leaves, one at a time, for about 15 seconds each, and transfer them to absorbent towels until needed.

4 SERVINGS

✈ GRILLED CHICKEN WINGS WITH SPICY HOISIN SAUCE

These chicken wings will have your guests coming back for more. The chili dipping sauce can be made 'a la minute, so you don't have to keep them waiting. If you can't find the wings completely intact (drumette and wing with tip connected), just grill the drumettes and wings as sold in most grocery stores.

Marinade:

3 tablespoons vegetable oil

3 tablespoons hoisin sauce

3 tablespoons minced garlic

1 1/4 teaspoon salt

1/3 teaspoon white pepper

24 chicken wings

Chili Dipping Sauce:

1/2 cup hoisin sauce

3 tablespoons tomato ketchup

1 1/2 tablespoons hot chili sauce

2 teaspoons light brown sugar, tightly packed

1 tablespoon minced scallion

2 whole scallions, sliced thinly on the bias

To prepare the marinade:
Place all marinade ingredients in a medium non-corrosive bowl, and stir to combine. Place the chicken wings in the marinade, and toss to coat. Cover the bowl with plastic wrap, place in the refrigerator, and allow the wings to marinate for at least 3 hours or overnight.

To grill the wings:
Preheat the grill to medium.

Remove the wings from the refrigerator and place on the preheated grill. Grill the wings for about 15 minutes over direct heat, turning frequently to prevent them from burning. Move the wings to indirect heat, and continue to cook for an additional 4 minutes until fully cooked.

To make the chili dipping sauce:
While the wings are grilling, combine all of the dipping sauce ingredients in a medium, noncorrosive bowl, and stir to combine. Transfer the dipping sauce to a serving bowl, set in the middle of a serving platter, and set aside until needed.

Remove the golden brown wings from the grill and place them on the serving platter around the bowl of dipping sauce. Garnish with scallions and serve immediately.

✳ **CHEF'S NOTE:** Keep the grill covered when cooking to impart a good smoky flavor and even cooking temperature.

12 SERVINGS

⟡ CHICKEN SATAY WITH SPICY PEANUT SAUCE

Add an Asian twist to your appetizer list. If you like, you can substitute beef fillet for the chicken and save time by making the sauce ahead of time. If you prefer a little crunch in your Satay sauce, use chunky peanut butter or add ¼-cup of chopped peanuts into the mix.

Marinade:

2 tablespoons sesame oil

2 tablespoons vegetable oil

¼ cup dry sherry

¼ cup soy sauce

2 tablespoons fresh lemon juice

1½ teaspoons minced garlic

1½ teaspoons minced ginger

¼ teaspoon salt

¼ teaspoon black pepper

1 dash Tabasco sauce

1¼ pounds boneless skinless chicken breasts

Satay Sauce:

4 tablespoons vegetable oil

2 teaspoons sesame oil

½ cup minced red onion

2 tablespoons minced garlic

1 teaspoon minced ginger

1 tablespoon red wine vinegar

1 tablespoon tightly packed light brown sugar

⅓ cup smooth peanut butter

½ teaspoon ground coriander

3 tablespoons ketchup

3 tablespoons soy sauce

1 tablespoon fresh squeezed lemon juice

½ teaspoon black pepper

1 dash Tabasco sauce

½ cup hot water

½ teaspoon turmeric (optional)

To make the marinade:

Place all of the marinade ingredients in a medium noncorrosive bowl and stir to combine.

Using a sharp knife slice the chicken breasts on the bias (diagonally) into thin strips measuring ½ inch wide by 2 – 3 inches long. Place the chicken strips in the marinade and refrigerate for 1-2 hours.

To make the satay sauce:

Heat vegetable and corn oil in a small saucepan over medium heat. When hot, add onion, garlic, and ginger, and sauté, stirring frequently until tender— about 2 minutes. Add vinegar and brown sugar and stir to dissolve. Remove the fragrant mixture from the heat and add the remaining ingredients. Stir to combine. Transfer the sauce to a serving bowl and set aside while grilling the chicken.

To grill the chicken:

Preheat grill to medium-high heat.

Soak as many wooden skewers as you have chicken strips, in water for at least 1 hour before grilling to prevent them from burning on the grill. You may use metal skewers instead of the wooden or bamboo varieties if you prefer.

Thread a strip of marinated chicken lengthwise onto each of the soaked skewers until all are threaded. Grill chicken skewers for 3 minutes on each side until fully cooked and tender. Remove chicken

skewers from the grill and place on a serving tray with Satay sauce. Serve immediately.

✻ **CHEF'S NOTE:** The best way to peel ginger root is to scrape the outside of the root with a spoon. If using a paring knife, be careful not to cut too deep, as the most powerful ginger flavor is immediately under the skin.

8 SERVINGS

✦ CHERRYSTONE "STUFFIES"

Chef Jasper White combines simple ingredients and the freshest shell fish and produces a New England favorite! The chef advises you may substitute bacon if pancetta is not available at your local grocery.

1 baguette (cut into ¼-inch dice)

¼ pound pancetta, chopped fine

16 cherrystone clams, scrubbed well in cold water

⅔ cup water

⅓ cup olive oil

3 tablespoons chopped garlic

2 medium onions (about 12 ounces), peeled, and finely chopped

½ teaspoon crushed red pepper

2 large eggs

2 tablespoons chopped fresh basil

1 tablespoon chopped fresh oregano

2 tablespoons chopped fresh parsley

⅔ cup grated Parmesan cheese

Salt and fresh ground pepper

6 tablespoons unsalted butter, thinly sliced

12 lemon wedges

To make the "stuffies":

Preheat the oven to 300°.

Place the diced bread onto a baking sheet and toast on the center rack of the preheated oven until completely dry—about 15 minutes. Remove from the oven and set aside at room temperature.

Heat a medium sauté pan over medium heat. Add pancetta and stir until slightly crisp—about 5 minutes. Transfer to absorbent paper towels and set aside.

Place the clams and water in a medium stockpot. Bring to a boil over high heat. Cover and simmer until the clams open—about 6 minutes. Strain the broth through a fine mesh strainer and set aside. Remove the clams from the shells and chop them into ¼-inch pieces. Set aside. Place the shells back in the pot, cover with water, and bring to a boil over high heat for a few minutes. Drain and reserve them.

Heat olive oil in a large sauté pan over medium-high heat. Add garlic, onions, and crushed red pepper. Stir until the onions are translucent. Remove from heat and cool.

To bake the "stuffies":

Preheat the oven to 400°.

Whisk 1 cup of clam broth with 2 eggs in a large bowl. Add pancetta, chopped clams, onion mixture, and chopped herbs. Season with salt and pepper and stir to combine. Add cheese and diced, dried bread and fold together gently.

Fill each shell with stuffing. Top with a slice of butter. Place the clams shell-side down on a baking sheet. Bake on the center rack of the preheated oven until the tops are golden—about 25 minutes. Remove from the oven and serve with lemon wedges.

✳ **CHEF'S NOTE:** To keep the clams from rolling all over the baking sheet or serving platter pour a generous portion of rock salt down first and set the clams right on it.

6 SERVINGS

✧ CHERRYSTONE CLAM SEVICHE

Chef Jasper White serves this easy yet sumptuous starter at his restaurant – Jasper White's Summer Shack – in Cambridge, Massachusetts. The ingredients are not cooked by heat but marinate in citrus juices and other seasonings.

12 cherrystone clams, scrubbed in cold water

3 large limes juiced (about 6 tablespoons)

2 jalapeño peppers, stem, seeds, and pith removed, minced

1 small red onion (about 3 ounces), peeled, root end removed, finely chopped

1 ripe tomato (about 6 ounces), skin and seeds removed, diced into ¹/₄-inch pieces

6 sprigs cilantro, chopped

Fresh ground black pepper

1 whole lime cut into 4 wedges

Crushed ice for serving

To make the cherrystone clam seviche:

Shuck the clams into a medium bowl with all of their juices. Clean and refrigerate 16 – 18 of the nicest shells for service. Remove the clams from their juices and chop them into small pieces — about 6 per clam — and place them in a medium noncorrosive bowl. Strain about half of the clam juices over them and discard the other half. Add lime juice, jalapeños, onion, tomato, and chopped cilantro. Season with salt and pepper, and stir to combine. Cover with plastic wrap and refrigerate 2 hours. Spoon the clam mixture back into the cleaned, chilled shell halves with plenty of juice. Serve with a lime wedge and cilantro sprigs on a bed of crushed ice.

✳ **CHEF'S NOTE:** It is very important that you get the freshest clams possible for this dish. The juice of the lime is what is actually "cooking" the clams, so the fresher the better.

4 SERVINGS

→ SPICY LITTLENECK CLAMS WITH RED BELL PEPPER AND TOMATO BROTH

This dish lends itself to being both a starter and an entrée. You could also use steamers, mussels, top neck clams, or shrimp, in this recipe. Either way, be sure to have a crusty loaf of bread on hand so your guests can enjoy the tomato broth down to the last drop.

2 tablespoons unsalted butter

2 tablespoons olive oil

1 small red onion (about 4 ounces), root end removed,
  peeled and diced into $1/4$-inch pieces

1 large red bell pepper, washed, stem, seeds, and pith
  removed, and sliced into thin strips 2 inches long

2 cloves of garlic, peeled, and minced

Salt and pepper

1 small, hot chili pepper, about $1^1/_2$-inches long,
  minced

1 cup dry white wine

6 pounds littleneck clams, scrubbed under cold running
  water, cracked, broken, or dead clams discarded.

2 medium tomatoes (about 8 ounces), peeled seeds
  removed, and diced into $1/4$-inch pieces

$1/4$ cup fresh chopped Italian parsley

Lemon and lime wedges for garnish

To steam the clams:

Heat butter and oil in a medium stockpot over medium-high heat. When hot, add onion, pepper, and garlic. Season with salt and pepper, and sauté until slightly tender—about 3 minutes. Add chili peppers and wine. Bring to a boil. Add clams, tomatoes, and parsley. Stir to combine. Cover the pot and bring to a boil. Reduce the heat and allow the clams to steam until they are all open—about 8 minutes. Adjust the seasoning of the tomato broth with salt and pepper. Divide the clams and broth mixture among 4 large bowls. Serve immediately with a few wedges of lemon and lime.

✳ **CHEF'S NOTE:** To check if a clam is dead or alive, tap two together. If you hear a hollow thud versus a sharp cracking sound the clam is dead and should be discarded.

4 SERVINGS

✦ SAUTÉED SOFT SHELL CRABS WITH BUTTERMILK CRUST

This southern delicacy is easy to prepare and a real crowd pleaser. In season, you should be able to find fresh, cleaned, soft shell crabs at your local fish market or specialty grocer. If not, frozen soft shell crabs are readily available and may be used.

8 soft shell blue crabs, about 4 ounces each, cleaned (see chef's note)

1 cup buttermilk

1 cup all-purpose flour

2 tablespoons chopped fresh parsley

1 teaspoon cayenne pepper

1 teaspoon salt

1/2 teaspoon fine ground black pepper

1/2 teaspoon dried thyme

1/4 cup salad oil

3 tablespoons unsalted butter

1 tablespoon chopped fresh garlic

4 large lemon wedges

To make the crabs:

Combine crabs and buttermilk in a medium bowl, and allow the crabs to soak for 15 minutes at room temperature.

While the crabs are soaking, combine the flour, parsley, cayenne, salt, pepper, and thyme in a shallow dish. Stir until well blended. One at a time, remove the crabs from the buttermilk, allow most of the buttermilk to drain off and dredge them in the seasoned flour, being sure that the entire crab has been coated. Set each crab aside on a platter until all 8 have been breaded.

Heat oil and butter in a large sauté pan over medium-high heat. When hot, add garlic and stir to incorporate. Sauté the crabs (top side down first) in the hot garlic oil and butter combination for 4 minutes on each side until crispy.

To serve the crabs:

Transfer the golden brown, crispy crabs onto a platter lined with absorbent towels, and allow to drain for 2 to 3 minutes. Serve the crabs with a slice of lemon.

✦ CHEF'S NOTE: If the crabs are not cleaned, use a sharp knife or kitchen shears to cut away the eyes and the face of each crab. Pull the corner of the top shell up to expose the lungs, and trim them away. Then turn the crab over and strip the bottom flap or "apron." Finally, place the crab on a flat surface and gently press the crabs' body with the palm of your hand from back to front pushing out the yellow bile or "mustard".

4 SERVINGS

✣ HERBED FARMER'S CHEESE WITH ENGLISH WALNUTS AND RAISINS

Farmer's cheese is a simple, fresh cheese made from what is left once the cream and butter have been strained off. The product is light, clean and very nutritious. Chef Daniel Orr likes to season it and serve it as a cheese course. The chef also uses it in dishes to replace creams and cheese that are more fatty in nature.

1 pound farmer's cheese, crumbled

1 teaspoon lemon zest

1 teaspoon chopped garlic

1 teaspoon Aux Poivre Blend pepper, cracked

1 teaspoon Mediterranean blend pepper, cracked

3 tablespoons chopped fresh chervil

3 tablespoons chopped fresh tarragon

3 tablespoons chopped fresh parsley

3 tablespoons chopped fresh cilantro

Salt

1/2 cup raisins

3/4 cup English walnuts, toasted

Grain melba toast

To make the herbed farmer's cheese:

Combine cheese, lemon zest, garlic, peppers, and herbs in a large bowl. Season with salt and cover with plastic wrap, and refrigerate for at least 3 hours before serving. Remove from the refrigerator, adjust the seasoning with salt and serve with the raisins, walnuts, and melba toast.

✖ **CHEF'S NOTE:** Farmer's cheese can be found at specialty groceries or gourmet markets as can Aux Poivre, a blend of fresh cracked red, green, black and white peppercorns. This simple dish is best served with balsamic reduction. This is prepared by simmering 1/2 cup or so of balsamic vinegar in a small, nonstick pan over medium heat until it reaches the consistency of maple syrup.

6 SERVINGS

✢ PRESERVED LEMON AND CUCUMBER SALSA

Moroccan preserved lemons, chilies, and cucumbers coexist in this delicious salsa created by Chef Daniel Orr. This is not only a great dip; it also adds depth of flavor, spice and a crunchy texture to a steamed fish entrée.

1 large cucumber (about 10 ounces), washed, cut in half lengthwise, seeds removed, and roughly chopped

1/2 fresh red chili pepper, seeds removed, and minced

1 teaspoon minced garlic

1/2 preserved lemon

2 tablespoons olive oil

1/4 cup chopped cilantro

Salt and pepper to taste

To make the preserved lemon and cucumber salsa:
Combine all ingredients in a large bowl, and blend with an emulsion blender briefly, being careful not to over purée or it will loose its texture. You can leave it as chunky as you like depending on what you serve it with. Adjust the seasoning with salt and pepper. Cover with plastic wrap and refrigerate until needed.

✳ **CHEF'S NOTE:** For a different flavor add a little chopped mint, scallion, Italian parsley, and 1/4 cup drained fat-free yogurt. The salsa can be refrigerated in a tightly-sealed container for up to 3 days; however, it will loose its bright green color after 12 hours or so.

1 CUP

⇢ MARINARA SAUCE

This simple tomato sauce is traditionally flavored with only garlic and herbs. The literal translation is "sailor style" sauce. Variations on the basic marinara, such as the cacciatore and pizziola sauces, are just as popular, flavorful and easy to make.

2 tablespoons olive oil
2 cloves fresh garlic, peeled, root ends removed, and
  sliced thin
5 pounds fresh plum tomatoes, washed, cored,
  blanched, peeled, seeded, and chopped into ¹/₂-inch
  pieces (reserve any juice)
¹/₄ cup fresh sliced basil leaves
2 tablespoons fresh chopped basil leaves
Salt and pepper

To make 1 quart of Marinara Sauce:
Heat oil in a large saucepan over medium heat. When hot, add garlic and sauté for 30 seconds. Add tomatoes with any excess juice and stir to combine. Bring to a simmer. Adjust the heat and allow the sauce to simmer, stirring occasionally until slightly thickened—about 40 minutes. Add basil and parsley and stir to combine. Adjust the seasoning with salt and pepper. Serve with your favorite pasta and grated Parmesan cheese.

→ CACCIATORE SAUCE

2 tablespoons olive oil

2 cloves fresh garlic, peeled, root ends removed, and sliced thin

1 red bell pepper, stem removed, seeded, pith removed and thinly sliced

1 yellow bell pepper, stem removed, seeded, pith removed and thinly sliced

6 ounces, button mushrooms sliced thin

1/2 tablespoon dried oregano

1 teaspoon dried basil

1 quart marinara sauce (recipe above)

To make 1¹/4 quarts of Cacciatore Sauce:

Heat oil in a medium saucepan over medium heat. When hot, add peppers and mushrooms, and sauté for 4 minutes until slightly tender. Add garlic and sauté for 30 seconds. Add herbs and the marinara sauce, and stir to combine. Bring to a boil, then reduce the heat and allow to simmer for 15 minutes.

→ PIZZIOLA SAUCE

2 tablespoons olive oil

2 cloves garlic, peeled, root ends removed, and sliced

1 teaspoon red pepper flakes

1 tablespoon dried oregano

1 teaspoon dried basil

1 quart marinara sauce (recipe above)

To make 1 quart of Pizziola Sauce:

Heat oil in a medium saucepan over medium heat. When hot, add garlic and sauté for 30 seconds. Add spices and the marinara sauce, and stir to combine. Bring to a boil, then reduce the heat and allow to simmer for 15 minutes.

✻ **CHEF'S NOTE:** It is very important not to brown the garlic, as browning it will cause it to become bitter and carry an unpleasant flavor into the final sauce. Also, be sure to select very ripe tomatoes for the best flavor in the finished sauce.

BEEF, LAMB AND PORK

⇥ BRAISED SHORT RIBS OF BEEF

The combination of braising and searing ensures the short ribs are nicely browned, and produces a tender, finished product with a deeper color in the final sauce. Remember to work with high heat when searing the meat.

8 6–8-ounce pieces of beef short ribs, bone in

Salt and pepper

1¹/₂ cups all-purpose flour

¹/₄ cup salad oil

2 tablespoons minced garlic

1 medium onion (about 4 ounces), peeled, and diced into ¹/₂-inch pieces

3 medium carrots (about 10 ounces), ends removed, peeled and diced into ¹/₂-inch pieces

3 stalks celery, washed, ends trimmed, and diced into ¹/₂-inch pieces

8 small red bliss potatoes (about 10 ounces), washed and cut in half

1¹/₂ cups chicken broth

¹/₂ cup tomato sauce

1 tablespoon dried thyme leaves

1 tablespoon cornstarch

2 tablespoons water

To braise the short ribs:

Preheat the oven to 350°.

Season short ribs with salt and pepper. Dredge the ribs in flour being sure to thoroughly coat all sides. Lightly tap any excess flour off each rib and set aside.

Heat the oil in a large sauté pan or braising pan over medium-high heat. When hot, sear the beef rib pieces for 3 minutes on each side until lightly browned. Remove the ribs and set aside. Add garlic, diced vegetables and potatoes to the pan. Season with salt and pepper and cook, stirring occasionally for 3 minutes. Add chicken stock, tomato sauce, and thyme. Stir to incorporate. Place the ribs back into the liquid along with the vegetables and potatoes. Bring to a simmer. Cover the pan tightly with a lid or aluminum foil, and place in the oven to braise until tender — about 2 hours.

Remove the pan from the oven. Gently transfer the ribs to a serving platter. Place the pan on the range, and simmer over medium heat. Dissolve cornstarch in 2 tablespoons of cold water creating a slurry. Slowly add the cornstarch slurry to the simmering braising liquid while stirring with a wire whisk until the proper thickness has been achieved. Adjust the seasoning with salt and pepper. Remove the thickened sauce from the range. Use a slotted spoon to place the vegetables around the ribs on the serving platter. Spoon some of the sauce over the ribs and the vegetables. Serve the remaining sauce on the side. Serve immediately.

✳ **CHEF'S NOTE:** It is very crucial that the pan has a tight lid so the sauce does not completely evaporate during cooking. The simmering liquid in the pan should reach half-way up the beef ribs to render them tender. Position the ribs on the bottom of the pan with the vegetables and potatoes in between or on top.

4 SERVINGS

⚘ CIDER GRILLED NEW YORK STRIP STEAKS

Do not add too much cider, as it will cause the steaks to start cooking too early. Use a cloudy variety of apple cider if possible. These are usually only available in the autumn, but you will notice a difference in flavor over the clear variety. If you cannot find apple cider, purchase mulling spices and spice up some apple juice.

1/2 cup cider

1 cup vegetable oil

3 medium carrots, peeled, ends removed, and diced into 1/2-inch pieces

2 medium yellow onions, skin removed, root end removed and diced into 1/2-inch pieces

5 cloves garlic, skin removed, and crushed

4 tablespoons pickling spice

1 tablespoon dry mustard

4 10–12-ounce New York strip steaks, fat trimmed to 1/4 inch

1 tablespoon paprika

Salt and black pepper

To make the marinade:

Combine cider, oil, carrots, onions, garlic, pickling spice, and dry mustard in a noncorrosive bowl. Place the steaks in the marinade and refrigerate for 1–4 hours.

To grill the steaks:

Preheat the grill to medium-high.

Remove the steaks from the refrigerator. Place the steaks on the grill diagonally and close the cover. Allow the steaks to cook for 3–4 minutes. Open the grill and rotate the steaks 90 degrees (to create the checkerboard-like marks). Close the grill and continue to cook the steaks for an additional 3 minutes. Open the grill and turn the steaks over. Cook on this side for 3–4 minutes. Open the grill and once again rotate the steaks 90 degrees. Close the grill and allow the steaks to finish cooking for 3–4 minutes. Remove the steaks from the grill and allow them to rest at room temperature for 5 minutes before serving.

⚘ **CHEF'S NOTE:** Choose steaks with bright red color and good fat marbling. Substitute the strip steaks with a porterhouse or even tenderloin steaks. Trim all but 1/4 of the fat from the exterior of the steaks to keep them from burning on the grill, and keep the grill covered when cooking to impart a good smoky flavor and even cooking temperature.

4 SERVINGS

⚜ GRILLED FLANK STEAK WITH ROASTED RED PEPPER AND SPICY JALAPEÑO SAUCE

This inexpensive cut of meat grills quickly and is quite versatile, depending on how you sear, grill and slice it. Use an instant-read thermometer to determine the doneness of the steaks (120°– 125° for rare, 140°– 145° for medium, and 160°– 170° for well).

3 tablespoons chopped parsley

1 small clove garlic, root end removed, and minced

1 medium red bell pepper, fire-roasted, charred skin, stem, seeds, and pith removed, and sliced into thin strips

2 small jalapeño peppers, about 1 1/2 inches each, stems removed, seeds and pith removed, and minced

4 tablespoons olive oil

1 2 1/2–pound flank steak, fat and outer silver skin removed

Salt and pepper

To make the sauce:

Combine parsley, garlic, roasted peppers, jalapeños, and 2 tablespoons of oil. Season with salt and pepper and mix with a spoon to combine. Set aside at room temperature until needed.

To grill the steak:

Preheat the grill to medium-high.

Season the steak with salt and pepper. Grill over medium-high heat for 6 minutes on each side. Remove the steak from the grill, and allow to rest for about 8 minutes before slicing.

Use a sharp knife to slice the steak on the bias, against the grain of the meat. Divide an equal amount of sliced steak onto each of 4 plates. Top the slices with roasted red pepper and jalapeño sauce. Serve immediately.

⚜ **CHEF'S NOTE:** Use food handlers' gloves when working with jalapeño peppers, as they are very hot and will burn your eyes and skin if the juice gets on them. Also, allowing the steaks to rest after being removed from the grill allows the juices to settle in the meat. It is important to slice the meat against the grain or the final product will almost be too tough to eat.

4 SERVINGS

✦ PAN-ROASTED PRETZEL-CRUSTED BEEF RIB-EYE

In this unusual steak recipe you will use the methods of breading, searing and roasting. Try it out when you want to impress your friends with a unique taste sensation.

1 16-ounce bag large, hard, salted pretzels, crushed into pea-sized pieces
½ cup Panko-style bread crumbs
2 cups all-purpose flour
3 large eggs, lightly beaten
4 12-ounce, bone-in rib-eye steaks
Salt, cracked black pepper, and garlic powder
4 tablespoons vegetable oil

To cook the rib-eye steaks:

Preheat the oven to 350°.

Combine crushed pretzels and breadcrumbs in a large bow. Toss to combine and set aside.

Place the flour and eggs each in their own large bowl.

Season steaks with salt, cracked pepper, and garlic powder on each side. One at a time, dredge a steak in flour completely coating the steak, and tap the excess flour off; then dip it into the eggs. Allow the excess egg to run off; then coat the steak with pretzel and Panko coating, pressing the crumbs onto the steak. Repeat this process with the remaining 3 steaks.

Heat 2 tablespoons of oil in a large skillet over medium-high heat. When hot, sauté the steaks 2 at a time for 3 minutes on each side. Transfer steaks to a large roasting pan or a baking sheet with sides. Repeat this process with the remaining 2 steaks. Place the sautéed steaks in the preheated oven to cook for 15 minutes, until medium rare — about 130°. Allow the steaks to rest for 5–8 minutes and serve.

✭ CHEF'S NOTE: It is not necessary to have bone-in rib-eye steaks; a regular thick-cut boneless rib-eye will work as well. You may also try this recipe using a porterhouse steak.

4 SERVINGS

→ PEPPERED NEW YORK STEAKS WITH PORCINI MUSHROOM AND COGNAC SAUCE

A steak lovers' dream, this hearty entrée, with its robust sauce, is the prefect meal to warm you up on a cold night.

Porcini Mushroom and Cognac Sauce:

3 tablespoons unsalted butter

¹/₄ cup minced shallots

³/₄ pound porcini mushrooms, quartered

Salt and pepper

1 cup beef stock

1¹/₂ tablespoons all purpose flour

2 tablespoons cognac

2 tablespoons chopped Italian parsley

New York Strip Steaks:

1¹/₂ tablespoons vegetable oil

*4 10-12-ounce New York strip steaks, fat trimmed
   to ¹/₄ inch*

Salt and cracked black pepper

To make the sauce:

Heat butter in a medium saucepan over medium-high heat. When hot, add shallots and sauté, stirring frequently for 2 minutes. Add mushrooms, season with salt and pepper, continue to sauté, stirring frequently for 4 minutes. Add beef stock and bring to a boil. Reduce the heat and simmer for 5 minutes. Combine flour and water in a small bowl. Stir with a spoon until smooth. Add the flour and water combination to the simmering sauce and stir to combine. Continue to simmer the sauce until it begins to thicken—about 8 minutes. Remove from the heat and set aside while cooking the steaks.

To cook the steaks:

Heat oil in a large skillet or grill pan over medium-high heat. When hot, season steaks with salt and cracked black pepper and cook for 4 minutes on each side until medium-rare. Transfer the steaks to a platter and allow them to rest while finishing the sauce.

Add the sauce to the pan that the steaks were cooked in. Use a spoon to stir the sauce being sure to scrape the bottom of the pan to pull up any remaining flavor left from the steaks. Simmer until a nice thickness is achieved—about 8 minutes. Add cognac and chopped parsley. Stir to combine. Adjust the seasoning with salt and pepper.

Serve the steaks whole or sliced on the bias into ¹/₂-inch thick pieces topped with some of the mushroom sauce. Serve immediately.

✳ **CHEF'S NOTE:** You could grill these steaks as well. However, you will loose the pan drippings that enhance the flavor of the sauce. Choose steaks with bright red color and good fat marbling.

4 SERVINGS

→ SLOW SMOKED BEEF BRISKET WITH SPICY BARBEQUE SAUCE

Use an assertive wood when smoking a tougher piece of meat, like this brisket. For presentation, pick garnishes that symbolize the flavors in the dish.

Spicy Barbeque Sauce:

1/4 cup olive oil

1 medium yellow onion (about 5 ounces), root end removed, peeled and chopped into 1/2-inch pieces

1 tablespoon fresh chopped garlic

2 large tomatoes (about 8 ounces each), peeled, seeds removed, and chopped into 1/2-inch pieces

1/2 cup apple cider

1/2 cup balsamic vinegar

2 tablespoons tomato catsup

1 tablespoon freshly chopped basil leaves

1 tablespoon spicy mustard

1 tablespoon tightly-packed light brown sugar

1 tablespoon hot sauce

1/2 teaspoon ground cumin

1/2 teaspoon ground coriander

The Rub:

2 tablespoons tightly-packed light brown sugar

1 tablespoon chopped garlic

1 tablespoon vegetable oil

1 tablespoon cider vinegar

1 tablespoon black pepper

1 tablespoon ground cumin

1 tablespoon paprika

1 tablespoon salt

1/2 teaspoon dry mustard

1/2 teaspoon red pepper flakes

1 large beef brisket, about 3 pounds

To make the spicy barbeque sauce:

Heat oil in a medium saucepan over medium-high heat. When hot, add onions and garlic and sauté, stirring frequently until tender — about 5 minutes. Add remaining ingredients and stir with a kitchen spoon to incorporate. Bring to a boil, then reduce the heat to a simmer and continue cooking for 30 minutes, stirring occasionally until reduced and thick. Transfer this hot mixture to the bowl of a food processor fitted with a metal blade and process until smooth. Cool the sauce in an ice water bath until cold. Transfer the cold barbeque sauce to a tightly sealed plastic container and refrigerate until needed.

To make the rub:

Combine all the ingredients for the rub in a small bowl. Use your hands to rub this mixture onto the brisket. Place the brisket in a plastic food storage bag and close tightly. Place the rubbed brisket in the refrigerator for at least 2 hours or overnight.

To cook the brisket:

Preheat one side of the grill to medium.

Load the smoker box of the grill with a couple of handfuls of soaked apple wood chips. When the chips begin to smoke, place the brisket over direct heat and grill for 12 minutes on each side to sear the outside. After the brisket is nicely charred on both sides, move it to the other side of the grill (the side that is off) to finish cooking over indirect heat,

turning occasionally until tender — about 6 hours. Continue to add soaked wood chips to the smoker box every hour to impart a nice smoky flavor.

Use a pastry brush to apply the barbeque sauce to both sides of the brisket the last 30 minutes of cooking. Remove the brisket from the grill and allow to stand at room temperature for 5 minutes.

Use a sharp knife to thinly slice the brisket against the grain and serve immediately.

✳ **CHEF'S NOTE:** If apple wood chips are not available, a suitable substitution would be cherry wood, or even mesquite. Keep the grill covered when smoking and cooking to impart a good smoky flavor and even cooking temperature.

8 SERVINGS

✦ STANDING RIB ROAST OF BEEF WITH ZINFANDEL CHILI-JAM

Chef Michael Lomonaco, owner of Noché Restaurant in New York City recommends this as the perfect all-American, all-in-one party meal.

Old Vines Zinfandel Chili-Jam Glaze:

1^1/$_2$ cups St. Francis Zinfandel

1 cup water

2 tablespoons tomato paste

^{1}/$_2$ cup black currant preserves

^{1}/$_2$ cup (8 ounces), dark brown sugar, tightly packed

^{1}/$_2$ cup balsamic vinegar

1 small onion (about 4 ounces), peeled, root end removed, and finely chopped (about ^{1}/$_2$ cup)

2 cloves garlic, peeled, root ends removed and crushed

2 whole, seeded smoked chipotle chilies or 1 4-ounce can chipotle peppers packed in tomato juice

2 teaspoons salt

1 tablespoon ground black pepper

Beef Rib Roast:

1 oven-ready rib roast of beef, bone in, approximately 4^1/$_2$ – 5^1/$_2$ pounds and 4 – 5 bones

^{1}/$_4$ cup olive oil

^{1}/$_4$ cup coarsely ground black pepper

3 tablespoons coarse salt

2 tablespoons chopped fresh garlic

3 tablespoons dry thyme

3 tablespoons dry rosemary

To make the Zinfandel chili-jam glaze:
Combine 1 cup of Zinfandel and the remaining ingredients in a saucepan. Heat over medium heat. Bring to a simmer; then reduce to low and cook for 20 minutes. Add the remaining Zinfandel and cook for 5 additional minutes over low heat.

To roast the beef rib:
Preheat the oven to 425°. Brush the meat with olive oil. Combine pepper, salt, garlic, thyme, and rosemary in a small bowl. Rub the mixture uniformly over the meat. Place bone-side down, in a roasting pan on the center rack of the preheated oven and roast for 20 minutes. Reduce the temperature to 350° and continue cooking for 1 – 1^1/$_2$ hours until medium-rare or an instant-read thermometer read of 130°. While cooking, periodically discard the fat that has accumulated in the pan.

Remove from the oven and let stand for 20 minutes at room temperature. Carefully transfer to a large cutting board. Lay bone-side down and insert a sharp knife between the meat and rib bones, separating the meat from the ribs in one large piece. Carve the meat into ^{1}/$_2$-inch thick slices. To carve into rib portions, simply slice each with a bone attached. Serve immediately.

✳ CHEF'S NOTE: The Zinfandel chili-jam recipe makes about 1^1/$_2$ cups and can be stored in the refrigerator for up to 2 weeks in a tightly-sealed plastic container.

7-8 SERVINGS

✦ WIENER SCHNITZEL WITH ROASTED RED POTATOES

This delectable Viennese dish renders the veal juicy on the inside, yet crisp on the outside. Its delicate simplicity allows each of the subtle flavors to shine.

Roasted Red Potatoes:
³/4 pound red bliss potatoes, washed,
¹/4 cup olive oil
Salt and pepper

Wiener Schnitzel:
4, 5-ounce veal medallions
Salt and pepper
1 cup all-purpose flour
3 large eggs, lightly beaten
2 cups bread crumbs
¹/2 cup clarified butter
4 slices fresh lemon
4 sprigs flat leaf parsley, washed and pat dry

To roast the potatoes:
Preheat the oven to 375°

Use a sharp knife to cut the potatoes into quarters. Place the potato quarters in a large bowl. Add oil and season with salt and pepper. Toss until the potatoes are thoroughly coated. Evenly space the potatoes on a non-stick roasting pan or baking sheet with sides. Roast in the oven until golden brown and tender — about 30 minutes. Remove from the oven and hold warm while making the Wiener Schnitzel.

To make the wiener schnitzel:
Line a flat, clean work surface with a 12"x12" piece of plastic wrap. One at a time, place a veal medallion onto the plastic, place another 12"x12" piece of plastic over the top and pound the medallion until it is very thin—about ¹/4-inch. Repeat that process with the remaining medallions. Season the thin medallions with salt and pepper. Dredge the medallions in the flour tapping off any excess. Dip the medallions in egg wash, allowing excess to run off; then coat with the breadcrumbs.

Heat the clarified butter in sauté pan over medium-high heat. When hot, sauté the breaded veal medallions until golden brown—about 3 minutes on each side.

To serve the wiener schnitzel:
Remove the golden schnitzel from the pan. Place an equal amount of the roasted potatoes on each plate place a schnitzel on top of the potatoes. Garnish with lemon and parsley and serve immediately.

✳ CHEF'S NOTE: You may substitute chicken for the veal in this classic dish. For an added flavor element, toss ¹/2-tablespoon of chopped fresh rosemary in with the potatoes and oil before you roast them.

4 SERVINGS

⇢ GRILLED VEAL CHOPS WITH YELLOW SQUASH AND ZUCCHINI

Veal is tender and doesn't need to marinate in acids to tenderize. To create symmetrical sear marks on the chops, place them on the grill on the diagnol and move them 90° after 4 minutes of cooking on each side.

¹/₄ cup plus 2 tablespoons olive oil

2 tablespoons fresh lemon juice

1 tablespoon minced lemon zest

1 tablespoon cracked black pepper

2 1-inch spring fresh rosemary

4 12-ounce veal loin chops

2 medium zucchini (about 1 pound), washed, ends removed and cut in quarters lengthwise

2 medium yellow squash (about 1 pound), washed, ends removed and cut in quarters lengthwise

Salt and pepper

To grill the veal chops and vegetables:

Combine ¹/₄ cup of olive oil, lemon juice, lemon zest, black pepper, and rosemary in a small bowl. Place the veal chops in the marinade and refrigerate for 2 hours or overnight.

Preheat the grill to medium-high.

Grill chops over medium heat for 8 minutes per side until the internal temperature reaches 140° on an instant-read thermometer. Remove the chops from the grill, and set aside to rest while grilling the vegetables.

Lightly brush zucchini and yellow squash with the remaining 2 tablespoons oil and season with salt and pepper. Grill zucchini and yellow squash for 3 minutes on each of the cut sides as well as the skin side. Transfer 2 pieces of grilled zucchini and 2 pieces of grilled yellow squash to each of 4 serving plates. Place a chop on the top of the grilled zucchini and yellow squash and serve immediately.

✷ **CHEF'S NOTE:** Use a vegetable peeler to remove the zest of the lemon, and take care not to remove any of the bitter white pith.

4 SERVINGS

→ OSSO BUCCO

This is an Italian favorite, and one that is worth spending time on. As suggested by author Elizabeth Riely of the *"The Chef's Companion"*, complement this delectable entrée with an equally fragrant risotto.

4 veal shank chops, about 1 1/4-inches thick
Salt and pepper
1 cup all-purpose flour
1/4 cup vegetable oil
1 medium onion (about 8 ounces), root end removed, peeled and diced into 1/2-inch pieces
2 stalks celery, washed, ends trimmed, and diced into 1/2-inch pieces
2 medium carrots (about 6 ounces), ends removed, peeled and diced into 1/2-inch pieces
2 tablespoons chopped garlic
2 cups chicken stock
1 12-ounce can chopped tomatoes
2 bay leaves
1 tablespoon minced lemon zest
1 tablespoon chopped fresh parsley

To braise the veal shanks:

Preheat the oven to 350°.

Season veal shanks with salt and pepper on both sides. Dredge each of the pieces in flour, being sure to coat the entire outside. Tap any excess flour from the shanks. Set aside.

Heat oil in a large sauté pan over medium-high heat. When hot, add the dredged shanks and sear the outside of the meat until golden brown—about 4 minutes on each side. Transfer the shanks to a large casserole or braising pan. Sauté onion, celery, and carrot in the same pan as the veal, and season with salt and pepper. Cook for 3 minutes stirring occasionally. Add garlic and continue to sauté for an additional minute. Add chicken stock, tomatoes, and bay leaves. Bring to a boil stirring and scraping any of the veal or vegetable essence off the bottom of the pan. Pour this liquid over the shanks. Cover the casserole or braising dish and place in the oven to cook for 2 hours.

Gently remove the tender shanks from the casserole, and transfer them to a serving platter. Transfer the braising liquid to a large sauté pan and bring to a boil over medium-high heat. Reduce the heat and allow to simmer until slightly thickened — about 4 minutes. Pour this sauce over the shanks. Garnish the platter with the lemon zest and parsley. Serve immediately.

CHEF'S NOTE: Sear the veal until it is very nicely browned. This ensures a tender finished product and deeper color in the final sauce. It is very important that the casserole dish or braising pan has a nice tight lid so the sauce does not totally evaporate during cooking.

4 SERVINGS

☀ GRILLED LAMB KABOBS WITH CUCUMBER, LEMON AND YOGURT SAUCE

The yogurt sauce in this recipe is a great low-fat accompaniment that compliments the Mediterranean flavors in the lamb.

Marinade:

1 small onion (about 4 ounces), root end removed, peeled and minced

2 tablespoons olive oil

2 cloves garlic, peeled, root end removed, and crushed

1 tablespoon fresh lemon juice

1 teaspoon ground cumin

2 1-inch fresh rosemary sprigs

1 1/2 pounds lamb, cut into 1-inch pieces

Salt and pepper

Cucumber, Lemon and Yogurt Sauce:

1 large cucumber (about 10 ounces), ends removed, peeled, seeded, and diced into 1/4-inch pieces

1 cup plain yogurt

2 scallions, washed, ends trimmed, and finely chopped

1 tablespoon chopped fresh parsley

1 tablespoon fresh lemon juice

1 teaspoon chopped garlic

1/2 teaspoon dried dill

Salt and pepper

To make the marinade:

Combine onion, olive oil, garlic, lemon juice, cumin, and rosemary in a small bowl. Season the lamb cubes with salt and pepper, place them in the marinade, and refrigerate for 2 hours or overnight.

To grill the lamb:

Preheat the grill to medium-high.

Remove the lamb from the refrigerator and thread an equal amount onto each of 4 skewers. If using wooden or bamboo skewers, soak them in cold water for 1 hour before threading and grilling meat on them to keep them from burning.

Grill the lamb skewers over medium-high heat for 6 minutes per side until the internal temperature reaches 120° on an instant-read thermometer. Remove the lamb skewers from the grill and set aside to rest while making the sauce.

To make the sauce:

Lightly salt the cucumber and allow to drain in a wire strainer for 30 minutes. Transfer the cucumber to a medium bowl and add yogurt, scallions, parsley, lemon juice, garlic, and dill. Mix with a spoon until well combined. Adjust the seasoning with salt and pepper.

Divide an equal amount of this yogurt sauce among each of 4 plates. Place a lamb skewer on the top of the sauce. Remove the skewer and discard. Serve immediately.

☀ **CHEF'S NOTE:** Select a nice red lamb shoulder or leg for this recipe. You may substitute lamb loin, which is much more tender, for shoulder or leg if you prefer.

4 SERVINGS

✣ PAN-ROASTED LAMB LOIN WITH BALSAMIC FIGS AND RÖSTI POTATOES

This entree demonstrates Chef Schimolers' love for simple techniques paired with the use of interesting combinations of flavor and textures. Search for a fine wine to enjoy this unique lamb and fig preparation with.

Balsamic Figs:

2 cups balsamic vinegar

1 cup dried black mission figs (about 6 ounces), stems removed, and cut in quarters lengthwise

1/4 cup granulated sugar

3 tablespoons fresh chopped rosemary

Salt and pepper

Rösti Potatoes:

3 large Idaho baking potatoes, peeled and covered with cold water

1 1/2 teaspoons salt

1/2 teaspoon black pepper

2 teaspoons fresh chopped rosemary

1/2 cup olive oil

Lamb:

4 6-ounce lamb loins, fat and silver skin removed

Salt and pepper

1 tablespoon ground fenugreek

To make the balsamic figs:
Bring vinegar to a boil in a medium, heavy-bottom saucepan over medium-high heat. Simmer until it reduces to about 1 cup. Add figs and sugar and continue to simmer for 15 minutes. Add rosemary and season with salt and pepper. Remove from heat and keep warm.

To make the rösti potatoes:
Preheat the oven to 350°.

Grate the potatoes in a food processor fitted with the large grating attachment. Transfer to a bowl and season with salt, pepper, and rosemary. Mix well.

Heat 1/4 cup of olive oil in a medium sauté pan over high heat. When the oil begins to smoke, add the seasoned potatoes in an even layer pressing firmly with a spatula. Reduce to medium and cook until golden. Use a large spatula to turn the entire potato "cake" over. Drizzle the remaining oil around the edge of the pan. Cook till the bottom side is also golden—about 5 minutes.

Remove from the heat. Drain any oil and discard. Bake on the center rack of the preheated oven in the sauté pan for 10–12 minutes. Remove and transfer to a cutting board. Cut it into 8 equally-sized triangles. Keep warm.

To roast and serve the lamb:
Season the loins with salt, pepper, and ground fenugreek. Heat 3 tablespoons vegetable oil in a large sauté pan over medium-high heat. When hot, sear until nicely browned—about 4 minutes on each side. Roast on the center rack of the preheated oven for 8 minutes. Remove and transfer to a cutting board. Allow to rest for 2 minutes.

Arrange 2 triangles of potatoes in the center of each plate. Slice each loin at an angle into 4 equally-sized medallions, and place on the potatoes, drizzle with balsamic figs and serve.

✣ **CHEF'S NOTE:** The balsamic figs may be made days ahead and refrigerated. Simply reheat in a nonstick sauté pan before serving.

4 SERVINGS

→ GRILLED RACK OF LAMB WITH TOMATOES AND OLIVES

Remember to place the racks of lamb presentation side down for searing. The markings not only enhance the plate, they also bring out the caramelization.

2 whole racks of lamb, Frenched

2¼ tablespoons olive oil

Salt and pepper

2 cloves garlic, peeled, root ends removed, and minced

1 medium shallot (about 1 ounce), root end removed, peeled and minced

¼ teaspoon crushed red pepper

4 large tomatoes (about 2 pounds), washed, core removed, blanched, peeled, seeded, and chopped into ½-inch pieces

12 Kalamata olives, pit removed and coarsely chopped

1 tablespoon fresh chopped oregano

1 tablespoon chopped fresh parsley

To grill the lamb:

Preheat the grill to medium.

Trim any excess fat from the lamb racks. Lightly brush the racks with 1 tablespoon of oil and season with salt and pepper. Wrap the Frenched lamb bones with heavy duty aluminum foil. Grill the racks over medium heat on both sides until the internal temperature reaches 135°—about 6 minutes on each side. Remove the racks from the grill and allow them to rest at room temperature while sautéing the vegetables.

To sauté the vegetables:

Heat the remaining 1½ tablespoons olive oil in a large sauté pan over medium high heat. When hot, add garlic and shallots and sauté for 20 seconds. Add pepper flakes, tomatoes, and olives. Toss them together until well combined. Bring to a simmer. Adjust the seasoning with salt and pepper. Add chopped oregano and chopped parsley and toss to combine.

Evenly divide the tomato and olive mixture onto 4 plates. Use a sharp knife to slice the lamb racks into 1-bone medallions. Place an equal amount of medallions onto each plate and serve immediately.

✷ **CHEF'S NOTE:** "Frenched" is simply a term that means the meat has been cleaned away from the end of a rib roast or chop exposing the bone. If you can't find Frenched racks of lamb, ask your butcher to do it for you. Use your favorite black olive for this recipe, but be sure to remove the pits.

4 SERVINGS

ROULADE OF LAMB FILET WITH PROSCIUTTO AND HERBS, ARUGULA, WHITE BEAN AND PARMESAN SALAD

Chef Daniel Orr, executive chef at Guastavino's in New York City, reminds you not to over-season the roulades with salt, because the prosciutto is already salty.

Lamb Roulade:

4 slices prosciutto

4 lamb tenderloins, gently pounded to an even thickness

3 tablespoons olive oil

2 medium cloves garlic, peeled, and minced

2 teaspoons chopped fresh rosemary

2 teaspoons chopped fresh thyme

1/4 teaspoon Chinese five-spice powder

1 teaspoon cracked black pepper

1 teaspoon lemon zest

White Bean and Parmesan Salad:

1/2 pound baby arugula

1/4 cup white beans, cooked and cooled

1 medium red bell pepper, fire-roasted, charred, stem, seeds and pith removed, and rustically chopped

3 tablespoons olive oil

1 1/2 tablespoons fresh-squeezed lemon juice

salt and pepper to taste

1/4 pound Parmesan cheese, shaved thin with a vegetable peeler

To make the lamb roulades:

Place the prosciutto on a flat, clean work surface. Top each slice with a pounded lamb tenderloin. Combine 2 tablespoons of olive oil, garlic, herbs, spices, and lemon zest in a small bowl and stir to form a paste. Season the lamb generously with pepper and a touch of salt. Rub the spice paste evenly over each tenderloin and roll, leaving enough prosciutto at the end to wrap around and seal each roulade.

Preheat the oven to 325. Heat the remaining olive oil in a medium nonstick sauté pan over medium-high heat. Sear the roulades on all sides – about 1 minute per side. Transfer to a small roasting pan and place on the center rack of the preheated oven to bake for 4 minutes. Remove and allow to rest at room temperature for 5 minutes. Make the salad while the lamb is resting.

To make the white bean and Parmesan salad:

Bring balsamic vinegar to a boil in a small, nonstick sauté pan over medium-high heat. Simmer until slightly thickened and reduced to about 1/3 cup. Remove from the heat and set aside.

Place arugula, white beans, roasted pepper, 2 tablespoons of olive oil, and 1 tablespoon of lemon juice in a large bowl, and toss to combine. Season to taste with salt and pepper. Portion an equal amount of salad onto the center of each of 4 serving plates. Using a sharp knife, slice each roulade in half diagonally and place on top of each salad portion. Add the remaining olive oil and lemon juice to those juices left on the plate that held the meat and spoon over the meat. Spoon a ring of the balsamic reduction around the salad on the plates and sprinkle with some Parmesan cheese.

✄ CHEF'S NOTE: The roulades can be rolled several hours or up to a day in advance. They don't need to be tied but if you prefer, you may do so with a small piece of string or a blanched leek strip.

4 SERVINGS

✦ APPLE WOOD SMOKED PORK TENDERLOIN

Smoking meat, poultry or fish is easier than most think, and it renders a very aromatic and flavorful result. Traditionally, more assertive wood chips are used while smoking meats and lighter, fruitier wood chips for fish.

2 tablespoons olive oil

1 tablespoon tightly packed light brown sugar

1 teaspoon ground cumin

1 teaspoon dried thyme leaves

1 teaspoon chili powder

1 teaspoon ground ginger

1/2 teaspoon cayenne pepper

2 pork tenderloins

Salt and pepper

To smoke and grill the pork tenderloins:

Preheat one side of the grill to medium.

Combine olive oil, light brown sugar, cumin, thyme, chili powder, ground ginger, and cayenne pepper in a small bowl and mix until smooth. Rub the mixture onto the pork tenderloins and place them in the refrigerator for 15 minutes.

Load the smoker box of the grill with a couple of handfuls of soaked apple wood chips. When the chips begin to smoke, season the tenderloins with salt and pepper, and grill over direct heat for 10 minutes on each side. Transfer the tenderloins to other side of the grill (the side that is off) to finish cooking over indirect heat — about 4 minutes.

Use a sharp knife to slice the smoked tenderloins against the grain into 1/2-inch thick slices, and serve immediately.

✼ **CHEF'S NOTE:** If apple wood chips are not available, a suitable substitution would be cherry wood, or even mesquite would work well. Soak the apple wood chips for at least 1 hour before smoking so they smoke and smolder in the smoking box. Put in dry, they will catch fire and burn. Keep the grill covered to capture the good, smoky flavor and ensure an even cooking temperature.

4 SERVINGS

✦ SOUTHERN STYLE STUFFED PORK CHOPS

A double-cut pork chop is more flavorful, and by stuffing with colorful and fragrant ingredients like cornbread muffins, chili peppers and flat leaf parsley, as opposed to regular bread and curly parsley, the end result will be a tasty and succulent chop.

6 medium corn muffins

2 ounces ($^1/_2$ stick) unsalted butter cut into
$^1/_2$-ounce pieces

1 small onion (about 4 ounces), root end removed,
peeled and diced into $^1/_4$-inch pieces

1 medium green bell pepper, washed, stem removed,
seeded, pith removed and diced into $^1/_4$-inch pieces

1 medium red bell pepper, washed, stem removed,
seeded, pith removed and diced into $^1/_4$-inch pieces

Salt and pepper

1 3$^1/_2$-ounce can chopped green chili peppers, drained

$^1/_2$ teaspoon dried sage

1 15-ounce can corn kernels, drained

1$^3/_4$ cup chicken stock

$^1/_4$ cup chopped parsley

4 12-ounce (bone-in) pork chops

To stuff the pork chops:

Preheat the oven to 350°.

Use your hands to crumble the corn muffins into $^1/_2$-inch pieces. Place the corn muffin pieces on a baking sheet and toast in the preheated oven until dry—about 18 minutes. Transfer the dried corn muffin pieces to a medium bowl.

Heat the butter in a medium sauté pan over medium heat. When hot, add diced onion and peppers, season with salt and pepper and sauté stirring occasionally until tender—about 3 minutes. Add chili peppers, sage, corn, chicken stock, and parsley. Bring to a boil. Remove from the heat and gradually pour into the bowl of dried corn muffin pieces stirring with a kitchen spoon until thoroughly mixed. Set aside.

To grill the pork chops:

Preheat the grill to medium.

Use a sharp knife to cut a deep pocket into each of the pork chops. Season the chops inside and out with salt and pepper. Stuff the chops with an equal amount of the corn stuffing, packing tightly. Grill the stuffed chops over medium heat for 6 minutes on each side. Move the chops to the upper rack or to indirect heat to finish cooking—about 4 minutes. Remove the chops from the grill. Allow them to rest for 5 minutes, and serve.

✳ **CHEF'S NOTE:** If you cannot find pre-made corn muffins at your grocery store or local bakery, simply prepare a boxed corn muffin mix. If the stuffing begins to get too dark during grilling, cover with non-stick aluminum foil for the remainder of the grilling time.

4 SERVINGS

→ GRILLED MAPLE-BRINED PORK LOIN WITH SAUTÉED APPLES

A potent solution of water and salt, used for pickling or preserving foods, is known as a brine. A sweetener like sugar or molasses is sometimes added to a brine. Brining adds both flavor and moisture to the cooked meat.

Maple Brine:

3 pounds, boneless, center-cut pork loin, fat and silver skin removed

1 cup warm water

1 cup apple cider

$^1/_4$ cup pure maple syrup

$^1/_2$ ounce fresh thyme sprigs, broken into $^1/_2$-inch pieces

1 tablespoon granulated sugar

4 tablespoons kosher salt

2 medium shallots, peeled and sliced thin

2 cloves garlic, peeled and sliced thin

1 tablespoon black peppercorns, cracked

Fresh ground black pepper

Sautéed Apples:

1 ounce unsalted butter

2 tablespoons pure maple syrup

3 Granny Smith apples, peeled, core removed, and cut into 12 equally-sized wedges

Salt and pepper

20 fresh thyme sprigs, about 1 inch long

To make the brine:

Combine all the ingredients for the brine, except the ground black pepper, in a large noncorrosive bowl. Stir with a wire whisk until the salt and sugar have completely dissolved. Place the pork in the brine, cover with plastic wrap, and refrigerate for 2 hours.

To grill the pork loin:

Preheat the grill to medium heat. Remove the pork loin from the brine and discard the brining liquid. Use absorbent paper towels to pat the loin dry. Season the pork with fresh ground black pepper. Grill the loin over direct heat with the cover closed until an instant-read thermometer reads 145° in the center of the loin — about 15 minutes per side. Remove the pork loin from the grill and allow to rest at room temperature while sautéeing the apples.

To sauté the apples:

Heat butter and maple syrup in a large sauté pan over medium-high heat. When hot, add sliced apples and stir to coat with the maple and butter mixture. Allow the apples to cook, stirring frequently, until tender—about 8 minutes. Place the sautéed apples in the center of each of 4 plates.

Using a sharp knife, slice the pork into $^1/_4$-inch thick slices. Place the pork on top of the apples, garnish with a few sprigs of fresh thyme and serve immediately.

❋ CHEF'S NOTE: Avoid using artificial maple syrup for this recipe, the 100% pure maple syrup renders the best flavor.

6 SERVINGS

SEAFOOD AND POULTRY

→ BUTTER-POACHED DIGBY SCALLOPS, QUINOA SALAD AND ORGANIC GREENS

Canadian chef, Judson Simpson has led his country's team to the Culinary Olympics and is Executive Chef of Food Services at the Canadian House of Commons. This is his original recipe and he uses quinoa, which is a grain that is light and cooked like rice.

Quinoa Salad:

1 cup quinoa

1 quart water

5 lime leaves

1 lemongrass stalk, cut into 4 pieces

1 2^1/$_2$-inch piece ginger root, peeled, and cut into 5 equally-sized pieces

1 tablespoon salt

5 tablespoons sultanas

1^1/$_2$ teaspoons minced ginger, blanched

1^1/$_2$ teaspoons minced lemongrass, blanched

2 tablespoons pumpkin seeds, toasted

4 tablespoons sweet corn, blanched

Sea salt

Dressing:

2 tablespoons fresh lemon juice

3 tablespoons canola oil

^{1}/$_2$ teaspoon granulated sugar

1 tablespoon minced shallots

^{1}/$_2$ teaspoon minced garlic

Sea salt and freshly cracked black pepper

Salad Bouquets:

3 tablespoons rice wine vinegar

2 teaspoons honey

2 tablespoons sugar

1 medium Daikon radish (about 7 ounces), washed and sliced on the bias into 10 slices measuring ^{1}/$_{16}$-inch thick, 1-inch wide, and 7-inches long

30 stalks asparagus, woody ends trimmed, peeled, cut into thirds, and blanched

40 mizuna leaves

30 3-inch long pieces chives

10 sprigs frisée

10 sprigs Italian parsley

Scallops:

4 tablespoons white wine

2 tablespoons water

2 lemongrass stalks, minced

1^1/$_2$ pounds small sea scallops, side muscle removed and discarded

2 pounds unsalted butter, diced into 1-ounce pieces, cold

Garnish:

1 pound coarse salt

3 tablespoons pink peppercorns

1 tablespoon finely chopped dried parsley

To make the quinoa salad:

Soak the quinoa under cold running water—20 minutes. Place 1 quart water, lime leaves, lemongrass, 3 tablespoons of minced ginger, and 1 tablespoon salt in a medium saucepan. Bring to a boil over medium-high heat. When boiling, add the quinoa and cook for exactly 12 minutes. Drain quinoa and refresh under cold water. Remove ginger and lemongrass and discard. Transfer the quinoa to a medium bowl and stir in sultanas, minced blanched ginger, minced blanched lemongrass, pumpkin seeds, and corn. Adjust the seasoning with sea salt. Cover tightly with plastic wrap and refrigerate until needed.

To make the dressing, prepare the radishes and bouquets:

Whisk all ingredients together in a small bowl and set aside.

With a wire whisk combine rice wine vinegar, honey, and sugar in a small bowl. Pour over the radish slices and marinate for 15 minutes. Artfully roll the remaining ingredients together into 10 small bouquets and set them aside until needed.

To cook and serve the scallops:

Heat wine, water, and lemongrass in a medium sauté pan over medium-high heat. Bring to a boil. Reduce heat and simmer until it has reduced by half. Strain and discard the lemongrass. Return the liquid to the pan and simmer over medium-low heat. Whisk in pieces of cold butter, one at a time, incorporate until smooth. It is very important not to boil this butter and wine reduction mixture. Hold the butter mixture at 165°. Poach the scallops in the butter sauce for 5 – 6 minutes on medium-low heat.

Toss the salad bouquets with dressing. Evenly portion the salad between 10 martini glasses. Place the poached scallops on top of the salad and drizzle with a little butter sauce. Place a salad bundle to one side of the scallops. Combine salt, pink peppercorns, and dried parsley in a large bowl. Evenly distribute this mixture onto 10 base plates. Put the martini glasses on top of the salt mixture and serve immediately with chopsticks.

✳ **CHEF'S NOTE:** Bay scallops would be a suitable substitution for the sea scallops. Adjust poaching time if your scallops are larger or smaller than 1-inch in diameter.

10 SERVINGS

✢ ALASKA SEAFOOD WITH COUSCOUS

Halibut isn't the only seafood that would work with this recipe. You could try this with pollack, cod, or sole. "Packet cooking" is a convenient, healthy and flavorful method of preparing individual supper portions.

4 12"x18" sheets heavy-duty aluminum foil

1 tablespoon vegetable oil

²/₃ cup cooked couscous

1 scallion, washed, ends trimmed, and sliced into
  ¹/₄-inch rings

¹/₂ cup sliced almonds, toasted

¹/₂ cup dried currants

1¹/₄ cups chicken broth

1 teaspoon ground coriander

³/₄ teaspoon paprika

¹/₄ teaspoon hot pepper sauce

4 6-ounce Alaskan halibut steaks

Salt and pepper

2 tablespoons unsalted butter, melted

1 lemon, washed, sliced thin, seeds removed

2 tablespoons chopped fresh parsley

To grill the seafood:

Preheat the grill to medium high.

Combine chicken broth, coriander, paprika, and hot pepper sauce, and stir until thoroughly mixed. Set aside.

Lightly brush 4 pieces of aluminum foil with vegetable oil. Combine couscous, scallions, almonds, currants, and half of the seasoned chicken broth, and stir to combine. Evenly divide this couscous mixture into the center of each of the 4 oiled pieces of foil. Place a halibut steak on each pile of couscous, season with salt and pepper, drizzle ¹/₂ tablespoon melted butter over the top of each steak, and top with slices of lemon.

Pull up 2 of the foil sides of each packet and bring them together. Triple fold the foil ends, creating a tube shape leaving about 1 inch of room between the foil fold and the fish. Triple fold one of the two open ends of the foil tubes so one end remains open. Add about ¹/₄ of the remaining seasoned stock into each packet, and triple fold the open end to close. Place the 4 packets on the preheated grill and allow to steam for 10 minutes until cooked.

Remove the seafood packets from the grill. Use a pair of tongs to open them. Be careful, there will be a considerable amount of steam ready to escape the packets as soon as they are opened. Transfer the mixture to 4 warm plates, garnish with chopped parsley and serve immediately.

✳ **CHEF'S NOTE:** Be certain that the stock is well seasoned with salt and pepper for a flavorful finished product.

4 SERVINGS

⤏ APPLE WOOD SMOKED SALMON FILLETS WITH SPINACH AND MUSHROOMS

Impress your guests with this delicately flavored dish. If you can't find the mushrooms specified in the recipe, substitute your favorites: chanterelle, wood ear, hen of the woods, or black trumpet would all add spectacular flavor to this dish.

3 tablespoons unsalted butter

4 medium shallots, minced

Salt and pepper

¹/₄ pound shiitakes, stems removed, and sliced
  ¹/₄-inch thick

¹/₄ pound medium white button mushrooms, quartered

¹/₄ pound oyster cluster mushrooms, torn into
  ¹/₄-inch thick strips

¹/₄ pound portobello mushroom caps, gills removed
  and diced into ¹/₂-inch pieces

¹/₄ cup chicken stock

¹/₄ cup dry white wine

2 teaspoons chopped fresh tarragon, plus 4 sprigs

¹/₄ pound flat leaf spinach (about 2¹/₂ cups), washed
  and spun dry

4 6–8-ounce salmon fillets

1 whole lemon

2 tablespoons olive oil

To make the mushrooms and spinach:

Melt butter in a large sauté pan over medium-high heat. When hot, add shallots, season with salt and pepper and sauté until translucent—about 2 minutes. Increase the heat to high. Add mushrooms, season with salt and pepper and sauté until golden brown—about 8 minutes. Deglaze the pan with white wine. Add chicken stock and bring to a boil.

Reduce heat to a simmer, and cook until the liquid in the pan has almost completely reduced and has a slightly syrupy texture. Add spinach and toss to wilt the leaves. Add chopped tarragon and stir to incorporate. Adjust the seasoning with salt and pepper, set aside and hold warm while preparing the salmon.

To smoke and grill the salmon:

Preheat the grill to medium-high.

Squeeze lemon juice over the salmon fillets. Brush the fillets with olive oil and season with salt and pepper. Load the smoker box of the grill with a couple of handfuls of soaked apple wood chips. When the chips begin to smoke, place the salmon fillets on the grill, skin side up. Close the cover of the grill and allow the salmon to cook for 3–4 minutes on each side.

Place an equal amount of mushroom and spinach mixture onto each of 4 plates. Remove the salmon fillets from the grill and place one on top of each pile of sautéed mushrooms and spinach. Garnish each fillet with a sprig of tarragon and serve immediately.

✳ **CHEF'S NOTE:** When picking salmon, select fillets that don't smell strongly and are firm to the touch. You could substitute striped bass or rainbow trout for the salmon as well.

4 SERVINGS

✦ STEAMED SALMON FILLET WITH LEMON AND THYME

Steaming locks the juices in and is therefore a wonderful and healthy way to cook fish without drying it out. Preparing the vegetables at the same time makes this not only a wholesome dish, but a convenient one as well.

1 tablespoon lemon zest

2 tablespoons fresh lemon juice

¼ cup extra virgin olive oil

1 cup dry white wine

1 bay leaf

1 small leek (about 6 ounces), green top and root end removed, chopped, and washed

1 2-inch sprig fresh thyme

1 teaspoon whole black peppercorns

4 6-ounce salmon steaks

Salt and pepper

1 red bell pepper, washed, stem removed, seeds and pith removed, and sliced thin

1 yellow bell pepper, washed, stem removed, seeds and pith removed, and sliced thin

1 head broccoli, washed, and cut into flowerettes

To steam the salmon:
Combine lemon zest and lemon juice in a small noncorrosive bowl. Use a wire whisk to vigorously stir the lemon juice and zest while slowly drizzling in the olive oil. Set aside.

Combine wine, bay leaf, leek, thyme, and peppercorns in a medium pot. Bring to a boil over medium-high heat. Reduce the heat and allow to simmer. Place a steaming basket into the pot. Season salmon steaks with salt and pepper. Place the salmon on the bottom of the basket top with the broccoli, and then the peppers. Cover and cook for about 8 minutes until the salmon and the vegetables are fully cooked.

To serve the salmon:
Evenly divide the vegetables onto each of 4 plates. Gently place a salmon steak on each portion of vegetables. Drizzle the lemon dressing over the top of the fish and serve immediately.

✦ **CHEF'S NOTE:** Any number of semi-flaky fish would be a good substitution for this recipe. Try cod, striped bass, grouper, or snapper.

4 SERVINGS

→ BLACKENED SEA BASS WITH LEMON AND CAPERS

Simple, quick and colorful, this dish has a little "kick" to it. While sea bass is a firm fish, remember to handle it with care and only turn the fish one time to blacken.

1 tablespoon chili powder

1 tablespoon ground cumin

1 tablespoon black pepper

1 tablespoon salt

1 tablespoon dry mustard

1/2 tablespoon ground mace

1 teaspoon cayenne pepper

4 6-ounce sea bass steaks

1 tablespoon vegetable oil

1/2 cup chicken stock

1 tablespoon fresh lemon juice

1 heaping tablespoon capers, rinsed

1 tablespoon unsalted butter

1 teaspoon chopped fresh parsley

To make the sea bass with lemon and capers:
Combine chili powder, cumin, black pepper, salt, mustard, mace, and cayenne pepper in a shallow dish, and stir to combine. Lightly dredge bass steaks in spice mixture, being sure to coat the entire exterior. Tap any excess spice off the fish and set aside.

Heat oil in a large sauté pan over medium-high heat. When hot, add the fish and cook for 3 – 4 minutes per side. Transfer the fish to serving plates and keep warm while making the pan sauce. Add the chicken stock to the pan to deglaze. Use a wooden spoon to stir the stock and lift any spices that are on the surface of the pan. Add lemon juice and capers; then simmer for 1 minute. Remove the pan from the heat. Add butter and swirl the pan constantly until the butter has completely melted. Add parsley and stir to combine. Spoon the sauce over each piece of fish and serve immediately.

✵ **CHEF'S NOTE:** You may substitute any number of firm-fleshed fish for the sea bass. Salmon, striped bass, snapper, or grouper would all work well.

4 SERVINGS

→ GRILLED SABLEFISH WITH GOLDEN PINEAPPLE CHUTNEY WITH GINGER AND APRICOT

The combination of nuts, fruit, spices and fish produce an aromatic Eastern flavor to this entrée. If unable to find sablefish at your local grocery or fish market, a great substitute would be dolphin or mahi mahi, both of which are readily available.

Golden Pineapple Chutney with Ginger and Apricot:

$1/3$ cup cider vinegar

$1^1/2$ cups granulated sugar

$1^1/2$ ounces fresh ginger root, skin removed, and cut into 1" x $1/8$" strips

1 teaspoon ground black pepper

1 teaspoon whole cumin seeds

1 teaspoon whole fennel seeds

1 teaspoon whole mustard seeds

$3/4$ teaspoon red pepper flakes

$1/4$ teaspoon ground allspice

5 ounces dried apricots, quartered

$1/4$ cup raisins

1 large pineapple (about 2 pounds), ends removed, peeled, quartered, core removed, and diced into $1/2$-inch pieces

$1^1/4$ cups walnut halves, toasted and coarsely chopped

Sablefish and Tomatoes:

4 medium plum tomatoes (about 12 ounces), washed, stem ends removed, and cut in half lengthwise

$1/4$ cup olive oil

4 6-ounce sablefish steaks

Salt and pepper

To make the chutney:

Combine vinegar and sugar in a large sauté pan over medium-high heat. Stir with a wooden spoon to dissolve the sugar. Add ginger strips, pepper, cumin seeds, fennel seeds, mustard seeds, pepper flakes, and allspice. Stir to combine. Bring to a simmer. Add apricot pieces and raisins and stir to combine. Simmer until the mixture has become quite thick — about 30 minutes. Add pineapple pieces and chopped walnuts. Stir to combine. Remove from the heat and set aside.

To grill the fish and tomatoes:

Preheat the grill to medium-high heat.

Brush the tomatoes and sablefish steaks with olive oil. Season both steaks and tomatoes with salt and pepper. Grill the tomatoes flat side down for 4–5 minutes, until nicely marked. Turn over and place them on the upper rack of the grill to finish cooking while grilling the sablefish steaks.

Grill the sablefish steaks over medium-high heat for 6 minutes on each side. Remove the steaks and the tomatoes from the grill. Place an equal amount of warm chutney in the center of each of 4 plates. Place the sablefish steak on top of the chutney, and place a tomato half on each side of the fish. Serve immediately.

✳ CHEF'S NOTE:

The best way to peel ginger root is to scrape the outside of the root with a spoon.

4 SERVINGS

→ BRAISED HALIBUT FILLET WITH SWEET RED PEPPERS, LEMON, AND CRISPY FRIED CAPERS

Traditionally, only muscle meats and tougher cuts of meat were braised. Now we braise poultry and fish as well. The colors from the vegetables in this entrée contribute to a vibrant and tasty presentation.

4 6-8–ounce skinless Halibut steaks

Salt and pepper

1/2 cup all-purpose flour

1/4 cup olive oil

1 small onion (about 3 ounces), root end removed, peeled and thinly sliced

1 medium red bell pepper, washed, stem removed, seeded, pith removed and thinly sliced

1 yellow bell pepper, washed, stem removed, seeded, pith removed and thinly sliced

2 medium tomatoes (about 8 ounces), skin and seeds removed, diced into 1/2-inch pieces

1/2 cup dry white wine

1/2 cup well-seasoned chicken stock

2 tablespoons fresh squeezed lemon juice

1/2 cup salad oil

1/4 cup capers, rinsed under cold water and patted dry with absorbent towels

1 tablespoon fresh chopped parsley

To braise the halibut:

Preheat the oven to 350°.

Season the halibut with salt and pepper. Dredge the fish in flour, being sure to thoroughly coat all sides. Lightly tap any excess flour off each steak and set aside.

Heat oil in a large sauté pan over medium heat. When hot, sauté the halibut steaks for 2 minutes on each side, until golden brown. Transfer the golden brown halibut steaks to a lightly greased medium casserole dish. Add onions and peppers to the sauté pan, season with salt and pepper, and cook, stirring frequently until slightly tender—about 2 minutes. Add tomatoes, wine, stock, and lemon juice. Bring this mixture to a boil. Reduce the heat and allow the vegetables to simmer for 3 minutes. Remove from the heat. Use a slotted spoon to evenly divide the vegetables on top of the fish. Pour the liquid into the casserole dish until it reaches half way up the sides of the halibut steaks. Cover tightly with non-stick aluminum foil and place in the oven to braise until the fish begins to flake when pressed gently with the back of a fork — about 10 minutes.

While the fish is braising, heat 1/2 cup vegetable oil in a small saucepan over medium-high heat. Bring the oil to 375°. Carefully add dry capers to the oil. First the capers will pop open quickly; then allow them to fry until they are crisp — about 1 minute. Remove the capers and place them on absorbent paper towels to drain.

Remove the fish from the oven. Use a large spatula to transfer the halibut to the center of each plate. Pile any excess vegetables that have fallen off the steaks back on top. Garnish with a sprinkle of crispy capers and chopped parsley. Serve immediately.

✳ **CHEF'S NOTE:** Sauté the halibut so it has a nice golden brown color on both sides. It is important that the casserole dish be covered tightly so the broth does not evaporate during cooking.

4 SERVINGS

✦ LINE-CAUGHT COD, BACON-WRAPPED ON A CREAMY LOBSTER SUCCOTASH

A classic recipe from Chef Jasper White. In the seafood market, the size you are looking for is referred to as chicken lobsters or 1-pounders. Chef advises purchasing lobsters that are lively and dark in color.

Creamy Lobster Succotash:

1 ounce unsalted butter

1 small onion diced into ¼-inch pieces

1 cup dried lima beans, covered with 3 cups cold water, and refrigerated overnight

2 1-pound lobsters, cooked, meat removed and chopped

4 ounces green beans, ends trimmed, blanched, and cut 2 ears corn, shucked, silk removed, kernels cut, and cob scraped to extract the milk (about 1½ cups total)

1 cup lobster stock

¼ cup heavy cream

1 teaspoon corn starch

1 tablespoon cold water

Salt and fresh ground black pepper

½ teaspoon cayenne pepper

Bacon-Wrapped Cod:

1 pound fresh cod fillet, cut into 8 2-ounce pieces

2 teaspoons fresh thyme leaves, chopped

Kosher salt

Fresh ground black pepper

8 slices country style bacon

¼ cup vegetable oil

2 tablespoons fresh chopped chives

To make the creamy lobster succotash:

Drain the liquid from the beans, and replace with an equal amount of fresh cold water. Place the beans in a medium saucepot and bring to a boil over medium-high heat. Reduce to medium-low and simmer until tender — about 35 minutes. Drain, season with salt and pepper and refrigerate.

Heat butter in a saucepan over medium heat. When melted, add onions and stir occasionally until tender—5 minutes. Add corn, lobster broth, and cream. Bring to a boil. Reduce and simmer for 10 minutes. Add beans and continue simmering for 5 minutes. Combine cornstarch and water in a small bowl. Mix until smooth. Add to the simmering corn-cream mixture. Bring to a boil. Reduce and simmer for 1 minute. Add lobster meat and green beans. Adjust the seasoning with salt, pepper, and cayenne. Keep aside.

To roast and serve the bacon-wrapped cod:
Preheat the oven to 425°

Season the cod with thyme, salt, and pepper. Wrap each piece with bacon; then thread 2 of the wrapped pieces onto each of 4 skewers.

Heat oil in a sauté pan over medium-high heat. Sear the skewers on three of the four sides until golden brown—about 1 minute on the three sides. Turn to the fourth side, and place the pan on the center rack of the preheated oven to roast for 5 minutes.

While roasting, ladle a generous portion of the succotash into 4 entrée bowls. Remove the cod from the oven and place a skewer into each bowl. Serve immediately.

✻ **CHEF'S NOTE:** Do not add the lobster meat or green beans until you reheat and are ready to serve.

4 SERVINGS

→ STEAMED LOBSTER WITH ASPARAGUS, FINGERLING POTATOES, AND GINGER SOY SAUCE

This steamed dish makes the perfect luncheon item. Healthy and savory, you could also serve this Asian-inspired entrée with a side of aromatic jasmine rice.

Steaming Liquid:

1 quart water

2 stalks of lemon grass

1¹/₂ ounces ginger root, about 1-inch long, peeled, and sliced thin

1¹/₂ ounces galangal root, about 2-inches long, peeled, and sliced thin

Lobster:

4 8-ounce Caribbean rock lobster tails, split in half

6 fingerling potatoes, washed, split in half lengthwise, and held in cold water

2 pounds asparagus, washed, woody stems trimmed off and ends peeled

Sauce:

1 cup soy sauce

4 tablespoons water

1 teaspoon minced ginger

¹/₂ teaspoon red pepper flakes

1 teaspoon sliced scallions

To steam the potatoes, lobster and asparagus:
Combine all the ingredients for the steaming liquid in a medium pot. Bring to a boil over medium-high heat. Reduce the heat and allow to simmer for 5 minutes. Place a steaming basket into the pot. Place potatoes in the basket, cover and cook for about 12 minutes, until almost tender. Add lobster tails, cover, and continue to steam for 3 minutes. Add asparagus, cover once again and allow to cook for 3 additional minutes. Make the sauce while the asparagus and lobster finish steaming.

Combine all the ingredients for the sauce in a small bowl, and stir to combine. Remove the lid from the pot, and portion an equal amount of the lobster, potatoes and asparagus onto each of 4 plates. Drizzle the sauce over the top of the entire entree and serve immediately.

✳ CHEF'S NOTE:

If you own an electric steamer, follow the manufacturer's instructions to steam this dish. A bamboo steamer works just as well. Most grocery stores carry frozen Caribbean lobster tails. If you prefer Maine lobster, separate the claws and tail from the body, discard the body and split the tail lengthwise.

4 SERVINGS

→ SAUTÉED RED SNAPPER WITH ISRAELI COUSCOUS RISOTTO AND ROASTED TOMATO VINAIGRETTE

Created by Chef Steve Schimoler of the Mist Grill in Vermont, this Mediterranean inspired recipe provides a great combination of flavors and textures. Several components are suitable for advance preparation allowing you to focus on the final stages of cooking the fish properly.

6 Red Snapper filets

14 plum tomatoes

12 cloves of garlic

½ bunch of fresh basil

2 cups of olive oil

8 oz of Israeli couscous

2 oz of butter

2 oz of red onion

5 oz of red bell pepper, washed and diced (medium)

5 oz of green bell pepper, washed and diced (medium)

5 oz yellow bell pepper, washed and diced (medium)

1 quart of lobster stock

3 tablespoons of fresh parsley, minced

1½ tablespoons of Dijon mustard

2 oz of balsamic vinegar

2 pinches (20 threads) of saffron, soaked in 1 tablespoon of water

6 teaspoons of salt

4 teaspoons of pepper

To make the roasted tomatoes:
Split the tomatoes length-wise, stem the basil and peel the garlic cloves. Place the tomatoes cut-side-up in a 3-quart baking pan. Add olive oil, basil, garlic, 3 teaspoons of salt and 2 teaspoons of pepper. Evenly mix, keeping the tomatoes cut-side-up. Bake at 350° for 35 minutes, until they begin to brown on the edges and are tender. Remove and cool for 15 minutes. Pour off the oil into a mixing bowl, remove the basil, half the garlic and 4 tomatoes and add to the mixing bowl.

To make the Israeli couscous:
Melt butter in a saucepan over high heat. Immediately add onions and peppers and sauté for 2 minutes. Add the couscous and stir well to evenly coat the pearls. Reduce the heat to medium and add all the lobster stock, 2 ounces at a time. The total cooking time will be about 10 minutes. Season with salt and pepper and add chopped parsley. Keep warm until ready to serve.

To make the vinaigrette:
Add Dijon mustard, saffron and balsamic vinegar to the mixing bowl that has the olive oil, tomatoes, basil and garlic. Using an immersion blender blend well until smooth and emulsified. Adjust the seasoning with salt and pepper.

To make and serve the sautéed red snapper:
Season the filets with salt and pepper. In a large sauté pan, add 2 tablespoons of olive oil and heat on high until the oil begins to smoke. Add the filets and cook until the filets are lightly browned and firm to the touch.

Spoon couscous on each of 6 entrée plates. Place a filet on top oand 2 half tomatoes on the side. Drizzle 2–3 tablespoons of the vinaigrette on and around the filet and plate. Garnish with some of the roasted garlic cloves.

✳ **CHEF'S NOTE:** Israeli couscous is a large, pearl-shaped pasta and is adaptable to many types of cuisine. If you can't find lobster stock, you can substitute fish or chicken stock.

6 SERVINGS

✦ CARIBBEAN STYLE CHICKEN LEGS WITH TROPICAL FRUIT CHUTNEY

The traditionally Indian flavors from the chutney mesh with the Caribbean marinade to produce an exotic yet easy entrée. If you add the fruit along with the yellow pepper and red onion, it breaks down as it simmers, rendering a smoother, less rustic, texture to the chutney.

Caribbean Marinade:

4 tablespoons apricot preserves

1 tablespoon Dijon mustard

1 tablespoon Walker Wood (or other) Jerk Seasoning

1 teaspoon curry powder

1 tablespoon salad oil

12 large skinless chicken legs

Salt and pepper

Tropical Fruit Chutney:

$1/2$ cup sherry wine vinegar

$1/2$ cup red wine vinegar

2 cups dry white wine

1 medium red onion (about 4 ounces), root end removed, peeled and thinly sliced

1 medium yellow bell pepper (about 4 ounces), stem, seeds, and white pith removed, and thinly sliced

$1/3$ cup clover honey

6 whole black peppercorns, cracked

1 large bay leaf

1 cup diced pineapple

1 red delicious apple, peeled, core removed, and diced into $1/4$-inch pieces

1 medium papaya (about 8 ounces), peeled, seeded, and diced into $1/4$-inch pieces

1 medium mango (about 8 ounces), peeled, pit removed, and diced into $1/4$-inch pieces

1 large navel orange (about 8 ounces), peeled, sectioned, and segments diced into $1/4$ inch pieces

2 tablespoons fresh chopped mint

To make the chicken legs:

Combine apricot preserves, mustard, jerk seasoning, curry powder, and salad oil in a small bowl. Stir with a whisk until smooth. Set aside while scoring the chicken.

Use a sharp knife to make 2 or 3 slices widthwise on each of the skinless chicken legs. Season the legs with salt and pepper and place them in a single layer in a casserole dish. Pour the marinade over the top of the legs being sure that each leg has been coated thoroughly. Cover the legs with plastic wrap and place in the refrigerator to marinate for two hours or overnight.

Preheat the grill to medium heat. When hot, grill the legs for 6–7 minutes per side, or until an instant-read thermometer reaches 165°, turning frequently to avoid over charring. Keep warm while making the chutney.

To make the chutney:

Heat vinegars in a large sauté pan over high heat. Allow the vinegars to boil for 3 minutes until slightly thickened and reduced to about $1/2$ cup. Add wine, yellow pepper, red onion, honey, peppercorns, and bay leaf. Bring to a boil, then reduce the heat and allow to simmer until the liquids begin to thicken slightly and the onion and pepper slices are tender—about 8 minutes. Add diced fruits and stir

to combine. Continue simmering until the chutney has thickened and become very glossy. Remove from the heat. Discard the bay leaf. Add the mint and stir to combine. Adjust the seasoning with salt and pepper and serve about ½ cup of the chutney with 2 of the Caribbean chicken legs.

✻ **CHEF'S NOTE:** The slices made in the chicken legs will help more of that Caribbean flavor get into the meat as well as reduce the amount of time they will need to cook on the grill. Bay leaves are not digestible, so remove them before serving the chutney.

6 SERVINGS

✦ GREEK CHICKEN WITH ARTICHOKES AND SUN DRIED TOMATOES

Convenient and bursting with flavor, this entrée is simple enough to prepare on a week-night, but translates into a beautiful dinner party presentation as well.

2 cups cooked orzo pasta

2 7-ounce jars marinated artichoke hearts, brine discarded, artichokes cut into quarters

1 8-ounce jar sun dried tomatoes in oil, cut into thin strips; reserve 1 tablespoon oil

1 3.8-ounce can black olives, drained

Salt and pepper

4 6-ounce skinless, boneless, chicken breasts, sliced widthwise into 4 strips

8 ounces feta cheese, crumbled

2 teaspoons fresh lemon juice

¼ cup chopped fresh parsley

To make the chicken:
Preheat the oven to 450°.

Place orzo, artichokes, half of the tomato strips, half of the olives and the reserved tomato oil in a medium bowl. Season with salt and pepper and mix until thoroughly combined. Evenly divide this pasta and vegetable mixture onto the center of a 12" x 12" piece of non-stick aluminum foil. Place sliced chicken breasts on top of the pasta. Season with salt and pepper and top chicken with feta cheese, and the remaining sliced tomatoes and olives. Sprinkle each with ½ teaspoon lemon juice. Pull up the foil sides and bring them together. Triple fold the foil ends creating a tube shape leaving about 1 inch of room between the foil fold and the food. Triple fold the sides of the tube creating a sealed packet. Place the 4 packets on a baking sheet with sides, and place in the oven to bake for 18–20 minutes.

Remove the tray of packets from the oven. Use a pair of tongs to open the Greek chicken packets. Be careful, there will be a considerable amount of steam ready to escape the packets as soon as they are opened.

Transfer the pasta and vegetables to a serving plate. Artfully arrange the sliced chicken breasts onto the pasta and vegetables. Garnish with a sprinkle of chopped parsley and serve immediately.

✳ **CHEF'S NOTE:** If you cannot find non-stick foil, use a heavy-duty aluminum foil instead. Spray the foil with non-stick cooking spray or lightly brush with vegetable oil. You can prepare this dish on the grill. Simply heat the grill to medium-high and shorten the cooking time to 14–16 minutes.

4 SERVINGS

✦ POACHED CHICKEN BREASTS WITH RATATOUILLE ORZO RAGOUT AND BLACK OLIVE MOUSSE WITH PINE NUT WAFERS

Created by award-winning cookbook author and chef, David Burke, this delicate chicken entrée is simple to prepare, yet guaranteed to impress.

Poached Chicken Breasts and Ratatouille Orzo Ragout:

1¹/₂ cups chicken stock

1¹/₂ cups tomato sauce

4 skinless, boneless chicken breasts (about 6 ounces each)

Kosher salt and fresh ground black pepper

1 large red bell pepper, washed, stem, seeds, and pith removed, and diced into ¹/₄-inch pieces

1 medium zucchini (about 8 ounces), washed, ends removed, and diced into ¹/₄-inch pieces

1 medium yellow squash (about 8 ounces), washed, ends removed, and diced into ¹/₄-inch pieces

1 small eggplant (about 6 ounces), washed, not peeled, outer 1¹/₂ inches diced into ¹/₂-inch pieces

1 small onion (about 4 ounces), peeled, root end removed, and diced into ¹/₄-inch pieces

3 cloves garlic, peeled, root ends removed, and minced

1 cup chopped fresh basil

2 cups cooked orzo pasta

¹/₂ cup grated Parmesan cheese

4 whole basil leaves

Black Olive Mousse:

¹/₂ cup black olives

1 small clove garlic, peeled, root end removed, coarsely chopped

1 teaspoon fresh squeezed lemon juice

2 tablespoons olive oil

1 cup crème fraîche

Kosher salt and freshly ground black pepper

Pine nut Wafers:

3 tablespoons vegetable oil

2 large baking potatoes (about 8 ounces each), peeled, thinly sliced and held in cold water

2 cups pine nuts, toasted

2 large egg whites, lightly beaten

1 tablespoon kosher salt

To make the pine nut wafers:
Preheat the oven to 325°

Brush a nonstick baking sheet with sides, with vegetable oil. Remove the potato slices from the water, pat them dry with absorbent paper towels, and lay them out onto the prepared baking sheet.

Place the pine nuts and egg whites in a small bowl. Season with salt and stir to combine. Spoon mixture over the potato slices. Bake on the center rack of the preheated oven until the potatoes are crisp and the pine nuts lightly toasted—about 12 minutes. Remove the wafers from the oven and hold warm.

To make the black olive mousse:
Place olives, garlic, lemon juice, and olive oil in a small food processor fitted with a blade. Pulse for 15 seconds. Add crème fraîche and continue to pulse until it begins to thicken and stiff peaks have formed—about 1 minute. Adjust the seasoning with salt and pepper and refrigerate until needed.

To make the ragout, poach the chicken and to serve:
Combine chicken stock and tomato sauce in a large saucepan over medium-high heat. Season with salt and pepper and bring to a simmer. Season chicken breasts with salt and pepper and add them to the simmering stock and tomato mixture. Simmer until the chicken has thoroughly cooked — about 5 minutes. Stir in the bell peppers, zucchini, yellow squash, eggplant, onion, garlic, chopped basil, and orzo. Bring back to a simmer and cook for an additional 2 minutes. Remove the chicken from the ragout and hold warm. Continue cooking the ragout until the vegetables are tender and the orzo is hot — about 3 minutes. While the ragout is finishing, slice the chicken breasts horizontally into 2 pieces. Spoon an equal amount of ragout into each of 4 entrée bowls. Place a sliced chicken breast on top of each portion, garnish with grated Parmesan cheese, black olive mousse, and pine nut wafers. Serve immediately.

CHEF'S NOTE: Ensure that the pine nuts for the wafers are not toasted prior to baking. Pine nuts toast very fast so keep an eye on them as they bake. If you prefer, use dried basil for this dish, remember to reduce the amount from 1 cup of fresh basil to 2 tablespoons dried.

4 SERVINGS

✦ CHIPOTLE RUBBED CHICKEN BREAST WITH ROASTED CAPPELINI CAKE

This seemingly simple dish has some delicate twists of flavor and presentation. Drizzle extra virgin olive oil on the plate just before serving to add a little extra flavor.

Cappelini Cakes:

1 pinch saffron threads

1/2 pound cappelini

1 tablespoon vegetable oil

1/3 cup minced red onion

1/4 cup brunoise red bell pepper

1/4 cup brunoise green bell pepper

Salt and pepper

1/4 cup chopped fresh parsley

1/2 cup grated Parmigiano Reggiano cheese

1/2 teaspoon fresh cracked black pepper

Chipotle Rub:

6 6-ounce skinless and boneless breasts of chicken

Salt and pepper

2 dried chipotle peppers, seeds removed and finely chopped

1 tablespoon paprika

1 clove garlic, root end removed, and minced

2 tablespoons vegetable oil

To make the cappelini cakes:

Bring 1 3/4 cups lightly salted water to a boil over medium-high heat. When hot, add the saffron threads and cappelini, and stir until slightly softened — about 1 minute. Continue to boil the pasta until it reaches the *"al dente"* stage. At this point there should be very little water remaining in the pot with the pasta. Strain off all but a few tablespoons of any water that has not evaporated during cooking, and return the pasta to the heat, stirring constantly until the water is totally evaporated. Remove the cooked cappelini from the range and set aside.

Heat 1/2 tablespoon of vegetable oil in a medium sauté pan over medium heat. When hot, add onions and peppers, season with salt and pepper and cook, stirring frequently until tender — about 4 minutes. Add the cooked pasta and toss to combine. Add parsley, cheese, and cracked pepper and stir to combine. Transfer this cappelini mixture to a non-stick cake pan so that it is at least 1-inch thick. Cover with plastic wrap and top with another cake pan, place something that weight about 2 pounds in the top pan to press the cappelini mixture into 1 tight cake. Refrigerate until cold — about 1 hour.

Heat the oven to 375°.

Remove the cold cappelini from the refrigerator. Remove the pasta from the cake pan. It should be one firm, solid mass. Divide into 6 equal-sized cakes with a sharp knife or circle cutter. Heat the remaining 1/2 tablespoon oil in a large sauté pan over medium heat. When hot, add the cappelini cakes and cook for 3 minutes. Turn the cakes over and place the whole sauté pan into the oven, and allow the cakes to finish roasting until lightly browned and hot all the way through — about 12 minutes.

To make the chicken:

Season chicken breasts with salt, pepper, chipotle pepper, paprika, and garlic. Use your hands to rub these ingredients into the breasts. Heat the oil in a large sauté pan over medium-high heat. When hot, add the chicken breasts and cook for 4 minutes on each side. Place the chicken in the sauté pan into the preheated oven to finish cooking—about 8 minutes. Remove the chicken and the cappelini cakes from the oven.

To serve the cappelini cakes and chicken:
Place a cappelini cake into the center of each of 6 plates. Use a sharp knife to slice the chicken breasts on the bias into 4 equal pieces. Place the sliced chicken on top of the capelinni cakes and serve immediately.

✳ **CHEF'S NOTE:** When cooking the pasta, the idea is to have the starchy cooking water reduce and make the pasta sticky. The starch in the cooking liquid is the main binding agent for the finished cakes.

6 SERVINGS

⤳ GRILLED TANDOORI STYLE CHICKEN BREASTS WITH RAITA

Traditionally baked in a clay oven, tandoori chicken can be served as an appetizer or an entrée. It is a low-fat, high-flavor dish and uses yogurt both as a marinade and as the basis for the sauce.

Tandoori Marinade:

1 1/4 *cups plain yogurt*

1/2 *cup minced yellow onion*

2 *tablespoons ground coriander*

2 *tablespoons minced ginger*

2 *tablespoons freshly squeezed lime juice*

1 *tablespoon curry powder*

1 *tablespoon chopped cilantro*

1 *tablespoon minced garlic*

1 *tablespoon red pepper flakes*

1 *teaspoon ground cumin*

Salt and black pepper

4 *6-ounce skinless, boneless chicken breasts, lightly pounded until* 1/2- *inch thick*

Raita:

2 1/2 *cups plain yogurt*

1 *medium red onion (about 6 ounces), root end removed, peeled and diced into* 1/4-*inch pieces*

1 *large carrot (about 5 ounces), ends removed, peeled and diced into* 1/4-*inch pieces*

1 *large cucumber (about 10 ounces), ends removed, peeled, seeded, and diced into* 1/4-*inch pieces*

To make the raita:

Combine all the ingredients in a medium noncorrosive bowl. Season with salt and pepper and refrigerate until ready to serve.

To make the marinade:

Combine yogurt, onion, coriander, ginger, lime juice, curry powder, cilantro, garlic, pepper flakes, and cumin in a medium noncorrosive bowl. Season with salt and pepper. Add chicken breasts to the marinade and refrigerate for 2 hours or overnight.

Preheat the grill to medium heat.

Season chicken with salt and pepper. Grill over medium heat for about 5 minutes on each side turning frequently to prevent them from burning. Remove from the grill and serve immediately with a few spoonfuls of raita.

✺ **CHEF'S NOTE:** Check the chicken breasts every 2 minutes or so. When grilling the yogurt-based marinade may get dark very quickly over the direct heat. If this happens move the chicken to indirect heat, to a higher rack, or simply reduce the heat. You could also sauté the chicken in a large non-stick sauté pan over medium heat for 3 minutes on the first side. Turn the breasts over, and place the whole pan in a preheated 350° oven for 8 minutes until the internal temperature reaches 165° on an instant-read thermometer.

4 SERVINGS

✣ ROASTED FREE-RANGE CHICKEN WITH ROOT VEGETABLES AND SHIITAKES

This is a quick, easy and colorful entrée, and has the convenience of being cooked in one pan, so it can go directly from the stove onto your table for serving.

Free-range Chickens:

2 3-pound free-range chickens, whole

2 tablespoons olive oil

8 cloves garlic, peeled, root end removed, and crushed flat

4 tablespoon chopped fresh thyme leaves

2 tablespoons chopped fresh rosemary leaves

1 teaspoon salt

1 teaspoon pepper

Vegetables:

3 medium parsnips (about 8 ounces), ends removed, peeled and diced into 1-inch pieces

2 medium turnips (about 10 ounces), ends trimmed, peeled and cut into 1-inch pieces

2 medium beets (about 10 ounces), ends trimmed, peeled and cut into 1-inch pieces

2 medium red onions (about 12 ounces), ends removed, peeled and cut

4 medium carrots (about 12 ounces), ends removed, peeled, cut in half lengthwise, and then into 1-inch long pieces

Salt and pepper

1 tablespoon unsalted butter

3/4 pound shiitakes, stems removed

To roast the chickens and vegetables:

Preheat the oven to 350°.

Use your hands to rub 1 tablespoon of oil onto each chicken. Rub garlic over the chickens; then place 4 cloves into each chicken cavity. Season each chicken with 2 tablespoons of thyme, 1 tablespoon rosemary, 1/2 teaspoon salt, and 1/2 teaspoon of pepper. Fold the wings under the backs of the birds; then use a piece of butchers' twine to truss the chickens. Place in a roasting pan and set aside.

Place parsnips, turnips, beets, onions, and carrots in a large bowl. Add oil, season with salt and pepper, and toss to coat. Arrange vegetables in the roasting pan around the outside of the chickens. Roast in the preheated oven, occasionally stirring the vegetables, until the chicken reaches 170°—about 1 hour. Remove from the oven. Hold warm and allow to rest.

Heat butter in a medium sauté pan over medium-high heat. When hot, add mushroom caps, season with salt and pepper and cook, stirring the caps occasionally until they are tender—about 6 minutes. Remove the caps from the heat and set aside.

Divide an equal amount of vegetables and shiitakes on each of 4 plates. Cut the butchers' twine from the chickens and discard. Using the same knife, gently cut the chickens in half. Carefully remove the rib bones and any pieces of the back bone, leaving only the drumette, leg, and thigh bones. Place 1/2 roasted chicken on each pile of vegetables and serve immediately.

CHEF'S NOTE: You may substitute regular chicken instead of free-range chicken, and your favorite root vegetables for the ones in the recipe. Remember to select hearty varieties of vegetables that can withstand up to 1 hour of roasting.

4 SERVINGS

→ ROAST LONG ISLAND DUCK BREASTS WITH VIDALIA ONIONS AND CRANBERRY GINGER RELISH

This entrée highlights the classic combination of fruit with game meat. The process of searing and roasting the duck breasts helps to extract the most flavor. An excellent accompaniment for this dish would be a generous portion of creamy polenta (page # 32). Simply place the polenta in the center of the plate under the duck breast and then top with the relish and onions.

Roasted Duck and Onion:

4 6-8 ounce Long Island duck breasts, skin on

Salt and pepper

2 tablespoons vegetable oil

1 large Vidalia onion (about 10 ounces), root end removed, peeled and diced into ¼-inch pieces

Cranberry Ginger Relish:

1 tablespoon vegetable oil

1 small Vidalia onion (about 4 ounces), root end removed, peeled and diced into ¼-inch pieces

1 tablespoon minced ginger

Salt and pepper

4 tablespoons granulated sugar

2 ounces rice wine vinegar

½ cup dried cranberries

1 cup fresh cranberries

To roast the duck breasts and onions:

Preheat the oven to 375°.

Season duck breasts on both sides with salt and pepper. Set aside. Heat 1 tablespoon of oil in a large sauté pan over medium heat. When hot, sear the duck breasts (skin-side down first) for 4 minutes on each side. Transfer the breasts to a roasting pan, meat-side down, and set aside.

Discard all but 1 tablespoon of fat that remained in the pan after searing the duck. Heat the tablespoon of duck fat (in the same pan the duck was seared in) over medium heat. When hot, add onion, season with salt and pepper and cook, stirring occasionally until translucent — about 3 minutes. Place onions on top of the duck breasts. Place the duck and onions in the oven to roast for 10 minutes. Remove the duck and onions from the oven and allow to rest at room temperature while making the relish.

To make the relish:

Heat oil in a medium sauté pan over medium-high heat. When hot, add onion and ginger. Season with salt and pepper, and cook, stirring frequently until translucent — about 2 minutes. Add sugar and stir to combine. Allow the sugar to begin to caramelize — about 1½ minutes. Add remaining ingredients and cook, stirring frequently until thick — about 2 minutes. Remove from the heat and set aside while slicing the duck

To serve the duck breast and relish:

Slice each duck breast on the bias into ½-inch slices. Place duck in the center of each plate. Top with an equal portion of the cranberry ginger relish and roasted Vidalia onions. Serve immediately.

✷ CHEF'S NOTE: This recipe produces a beautiful medium-rare duck breast. Long Island duck breasts are very large; almost twice the size of other types. You may use another type, but reduce the cooking time accordingly.

4 SERVINGS

☆ SAUSAGE AND HAZELNUT STUFFED TURKEY BREAST WITH MADEIRA GRAVY

This boneless stuffed breast is brimming with fruits, nuts and sausge - certainly not your mother's Thanksgiving turkey!

Sausage and Hazelnut Stuffing:

1 turkey tenderloin, diced

4 ounces fresh pork sausage

2 ounces unsalted butter

1 small yellow onion (about 4 ounces), root end removed, peeled and diced into 1/4-inch pieces

1 stalk celery, washed, ends trimmed, and diced into 1/4-inch pieces

Salt and pepper

1 small red delicious apple (about 4 ounces), washed, core removed, and diced into 1/4-inch pieces

1 ounce diced cooked ham

2 ounces dried apricots, diced into 1/4-inch pieces

1 teaspoon chopped fresh sage

1 tablespoon chopped fresh parsley

3 large eggs

1/2 cup heavy cream

2 ounces fresh bread, diced into 1/4-inch pieces

1/4 cup chopped toasted hazelnuts

Turkey:

1 fresh, skinless and boneless turkey breast

Salt and pepper

1 tablespoon vegetable oil

Madeira Gravy:

2 cups turkey stock

1/4 cup Madeira

2 1/2 tablespoons flour

To make the sausage and hazelnut stuffing:

Heat a medium sauté pan over medium heat. When hot, add sausage and cook, breaking it up into 1/4-inch pieces as it cooks until done — about 4 minutes. Transfer the sausage to absorbent towels. Cook the turkey pieces in the hot sausage fat stirring frequently until tender — about 5 minutes. Transfer them to absorbent towels and discard the fat. Heat the butter in a medium sauté pan over medium heat. When hot, add onion and celery, season with salt and pepper and cook until tender — about 5 minutes. Combine all the stuffing ingredients together in a large bowl and mix with a kitchen spoon to combine. Adjust the seasoning with salt and pepper. Set aside.

To stuff and cook the turkey breast:

Use a sharp knife to cut a large opening in the turkey breast lengthwise from end to end. Pack stuffing into the cavity, and tie the breast up with butchers' twine to hold together. Season the turkey breast with salt and pepper. Heat oil in a large sauté pan over medium-high heat. When hot, sear the turkey breast on all sides until golden brown. Transfer the breast to a roasting pan, and roast in the oven until fully cooked and tender — about 24 minutes. Remove the roasted breast from the oven and allow to rest while making the Madeira gravy.

To make the Madeira gravy:

Deglaze the roasting pan with turkey stock over high heat on the range, scraping the bottom of the pan with a wooden spoon to release any pan drippings. Bring stock to a boil. Combine the Madeira and flour creating a smooth slurry. Add this slurry to the boiling turkey stock and whisk until smooth. Allow the gravy to boil until nicely thickened. Adjust the seasoning with salt and pepper.

Place about 3 ounces of hot gravy in the center of each of 4 plates. Using a sharp knife, slice the stuffed turkey breast on the bias into 8 slices. Place 2 slices on top of each pool of sauce, and serve immediately.

✳ **CHEF'S NOTE:** You may substitute chicken stock for turkey stock. If you have the giblets from the turkey, place them in the roasting pan with the breast, they will add drippings to the pan, and make a deeper, better tasting gravy. Remember to discard them before deglazing with the stock.

4 SERVINGS

✣ CAJUN-BRINED SMOKED TURKEY

This recipes calls for a rubbed brine that adds flavor and moisture, but remember too much rub will end up burning on the bird. Ensure the center pan is full of boiling water as the turkey cooks, steam helps produce a very moist, finished turkey.

Chili Rub:

1/2 cup chili powder

1/4 cup (4 ounces) tightly packed light brown sugar

1/4 cup kosher salt

1 whole turkey (about 10–12 pounds)

Cajun Brine:

1 12-ounce bottle of your favorite beer

1/2 cup clover honey

1/2 cup dry Cajun style seasoning

1/3 cup hot pepper sauce

1/4 cup apple cider

2 tablespoon Worcestershire sauce

1 tablespoon salt

1 teaspoon ground allspice

To make the rub:

Combine chili powder, brown sugar, and salt in a small bowl, and mix with your fingers until well blended. Set aside.

Remove giblet bag and neck from the turkey and discard. Thoroughly rinse the bird inside and out under cold running water. Pat dry, inside and out, with absorbent toweling. Use your hands to apply the chili rub inside and outside the bird.

Tightly cover the chili-rubbed turkey with plastic wrap and refrigerate for 2 hours or overnight.

To make the Cajun brine:

Place all the ingredients for the brine in a medium bowl. Whisk the ingredients until thor-

oughly combined. Use an injector to pump the brine into the breasts, thighs, and legs. Using even squeezing pressure on the plunger and a smooth back and forth motion, be sure to inject brine evenly throughout the entire bird. Refrigerate for at least 2 hours.

To smoke cook the turkey:

Preheat the smoker/grill to medium-hot. Fill the pan in the center with boiling water. Place the brined turkey on the top rack of the smoker and close the lid. Open the door on the side of the smoker to access the hot coals. Place a couple of handfuls of soaked apple wood chips on the hot coals closest to the door opening. Close the door and allow the turkey to smoke and begin cooking for 30 minutes. Open the side door again and add more chips. Close the door and continue cooking until the turkey is tender and the internal temperature has reached 170°–180° on an instant-read thermometer — about 1 1/2 hours.

Remove from the smoker and allow to rest at room temperature for about 8–10 minutes. Use a very sharp knife to slice the turkey, and serve immediately.

✳ **CHEF'S NOTE:** Stoke (add charcoal to) the fire every half-hour to maintain an even cooking temperature. To stoke, simply sprinkle a dozen or so pieces of charcoal over the hot coals.

10 –12 SERVINGS

⟡ ONTARIO TURKEY TENDERLOIN WITH A MUSHROOM MANTEL

Canadian chef, Jud Simpson, creates a unique yet simple turkey tenderloin. The blueberry sauce is an unexpected surprise, but the perfect compliment to the flavours of the mushrooms.

Ontario Turkey Tenderloin:

$1^{1}/_{2}$ ounces unsalted butter, cut into $^{1}/_{2}$-ounce pieces

1 large shallot, peeled, root end removed, and minced

$^{1}/_{4}$ pound chantrelle mushrooms, sliced thin

$^{1}/_{4}$ pound morel mushrooms, sliced into quarters lengthwise

Salt and pepper

3 teaspoons fresh chopped thyme

$4^{1}/_{2}$ pounds turkey tenderloin, $^{3}/_{4}$ pounds of the thin tail ends removed and chopped into $^{1}/_{2}$-inch pieces

1 large egg white

$^{3}/_{4}$ cup half-and-half cream

3 tablespoons chopped fresh parsley

1 tablespoon pink peppercorns, cracked

1 tablespoon black peppercorns, cracked

Blueberry Sauce:

1 tablespoon unsalted butter

1 medium shallot, peeled, root end removed, and minced

1 cup blueberries, stems removed

$^{1}/_{4}$ cup raspberry vinegar

$1^{1}/_{2}$ cups reduced chicken stock

1 teaspoon chopped fresh sage

Salt and Pepper

To make the Ontario turkey tenderloin:

Heat a large sauté pan over medium-high heat. When hot, add butter and lightly brown—about 20 seconds. Add shallots and sauté until tender — about $1^{1}/_{2}$ minutes. Add mushrooms and season with salt, pepper, and 1 teaspoon of thyme. Stir frequently until tender — about 4 minutes. Transfer to a dinner plate and refrigerate until cold.

Place the $^{3}/_{4}$ pound turkey trimmings, egg white, and half-and-half in the bowl of a food processor fitted with a metal blade. Pulse for 15 seconds and process until smooth. Transfer to a medium bowl. Add the cold mushrooms and fold together with a rubber spatula. Adjust the seasoning with salt and pepper. Transfer this mixture to a pastry bag fitted with a straight tip and refrigerate until needed.

Lay a large piece of plastic wrap out on a clean, dry work surface. Sprinkle with chopped parsley, peppercorns, salt, and the remaining thyme. Place the tenderloin on the plastic wrap, pipe the pureed turkey mixture on top, and spread evenly. Wrap tightly with plastic wrap and refrigerate until ready to poach. Simmer 2 quarts of water in a large stockpot over medium heat. When simmering, place the wrapped turkey in the water and poach until the internal temperature reaches 140°. Remove from the poaching liquid and rest at room temperature while preparing the blueberry sauce — about 5 minutes.

To make the blueberry sauce:

Heat butter in a medium saucepan over medium-high heat. When melted, add shallots and sauté until translucent — about 3 minutes. Stir in the blueberries and raspberry vinegar. Bring to a simmer and cook for 1 minute. Add reduced chicken stock and sage, and continue to simmer until the sauce reduces by $1/3$ and thickens slightly. Adjust the seasoning with salt and pepper.

Use a sharp knife to slice the turkey on the bias into $3/4$-inch thick slices. Present with whipped potatoes and vegetables of your choice. Drizzle with blueberry sauce and serve immediately.

✳ **CHEF'S NOTE:** To prepare a good reduced chicken stock, reduce $2^1/2$ gallons of good quality, unsalted stock down to 1 quart.

10 SERVINGS

→ BRAISED GUINEA HEN WITH PANCETTA, MORELS AND HERBED POLENTA

One of Chef Michael Lomonaco's favorites, this entrée has a distinctly Tuscan flavor to it. The polenta may be served soft, or poured into a cookie tin and chilled until firm; then cut into squares and grilled.

Soft Herbed Polenta:

2 cups whole milk

1 cup cold water

$^1/_2$ teaspoon salt

1 cup cornmeal

$^1/_2$ stick (2 ounces), unsalted butter, cut into $^1/_2$-ounce pieces

3 tablespoons freshly grated Parmesan cheese

3 tablespoons chopped fresh herbs, such as thyme, parsley and chives

Braised Guinea hen with Pancetta and Morels:

2 tablespoons olive oil

$^1/_2$ pound Italian pancetta, soaked and cut into $^1/_4$-inch cubes

2 cloves garlic, peeled, root ends removed

1 leek, white portion only, root end removed, washed, and thinly sliced

2 small white onions (about 6 ounces), peeled, root ends removed and finely chopped

Salt and pepper

4 guinea hen breasts (about 8 ounces each), breast bone removed and wing bone attached

3 tablespoons all-purpose flour

1 cup fresh morel mushrooms, cleaned and quartered

2 young carrots (about 4 ounces), peeled, ends removed and thinly sliced

$^1/_2$ cup red wine, Sangiovese preferred

1 cup chicken stock

3 tablespoons unsalted butter, cut into ?-ounce pieces

2 tablespoons fresh thyme

To make the soft herbed polenta:

Combine milk, water, salt, and cornmeal in a medium, heavy-gauge saucepan. Whisk to eliminate any lumps. Bring to a boil over medium-high heat. Reduce to very low and simmer for 25 minutes, stirring occasionally with a wooden spoon. Remove from the heat and add butter, Parmesan cheese and herbs. Stir quickly to incorporate. Hold warm while braising the guinea hens.

To braise the Guinea hen:

Heat a 2-inch deep, lidded, skillet or sauté pan over medium heat. When hot, add olive oil and pancetta. Stir occasionally until evenly browned — about 6 minutes. Add garlic, leeks, and onions and sauté until they begin to caramelize—about 5 minutes. Remove the leeks and onions and set aside, reserve the drippings for cooking the hens.

Season the hen breasts with salt and pepper, dredge in flour tapping any excess off. Sauté in the skillet used for the pancetta and vegetables. Sear over medium-high heat until brown—about 4 minutes on each side. Add mushrooms and carrots and cook for 2 minutes. Return the leek-onion mixture to the pan. Add wine and allow it to reduce for 1 minute. Add stock to the pan and bring to a boil. Reduce the heat to low, cover tightly with a lid, and simmer. Braise for 7–8 minutes or until the hen is fully cooked.

When the braising liquid has reduced by half and the hens are sufficiently cooked, remove and place on a platter, add butter to the pan juices and whisk to combine. Add fresh thyme leaves and serve immediately on a bed of polenta, with some vegetable and herb pan juices spooned over the top.

✳ **CHEF'S NOTE:** If, toward the end of the cooking, the polenta is too thick and heavy to stir, add one or more tablespoons of cold water to loosen the mixture, and maintain a creamy consistency.

4 SERVINGS

⇾ SAUTÉED BREAST OF PHEASANT WITH ORANGE SEGMENTS AND PORT WINE GLAZE

Pheasant breasts may be difficult to find, but your specialty grocer or butcher should be able to get them for you. If not, try guinea hen breasts or chicken breasts. The pheasant breasts give the recipe an enhanced flavor and are worth the effort for a special occasion.

4 skinless boneless pheasant breasts,
  each about 6 ounces
Salt and pepper
1/4 cup all-purpose flour
2 tablespoons salad oil
1 small onion (about 4 ounces), skin and root end
  removed, and diced into 1/4-inch pieces
1/2 cup port wine
1 teaspoon granulated sugar
1/2 teaspoon ground cinnamon
2 tablespoons unsalted butter
1 teaspoon chopped fresh parsley
2 medium oranges (about 10 ounces) peeled, and
  segmented, and juices reserved
1/2 cup fresh raspberries

To make the sautéed pheasant with oranges and port wine glaze:

Season pheasant breasts with salt and pepper. Dredge the breasts in flour and tap off any excess. Heat 1 tablespoon of oil in a sauté pan over medium-high heat. When hot, sauté the pheasant for 4 minutes on each side. Transfer the breasts to a platter and keep warm while preparing the sauce.

Heat remaining oil in the same pan and sauté the onion until light brown — about 3 minutes. Add port, sugar, cinnamon, and the reserved orange juice. Bring to a boil. Reduce the heat and simmer for 1 minute. Remove the pan from the heat. Add butter and swirl the pan constantly until completely incorporated. Add parsley, orange segments, and raspberries to the sauce and swirl to combine.

Place a pheasant breast onto each of 4 plates. Top each breast with some of the fruit sauce and serve immediately.

✴ **CHEF'S NOTE:** Be sure to add the fruit at the last minute so it doesn't break down too fast.

4 SERVINGS

BREADS AND DESSERTS

✦ CINNAMON BUNS

Let your taste buds and imagination run wild by using a variety of toppings on these sweet breads. Egg wash can be substituted for the melted butter on the cinnamon buns, and is a lower-fat alternative.

Sweet Dough:

$6^1/_2$ tablespoons granulated sugar

1 teaspoon salt

$5^1/_2$ tablespoons vegetable shortening

1 large egg, lightly beaten

1 teaspoon lemon extract

$3^1/_2$ cups all-purpose flour

2 teaspoons instant yeast

$1^1/_4$ cups whole milk

1 teaspoon vegetable oil

Cinnamon Buns:

1 cup all-purpose flour

$6^1/_2$ tablespoons granulated sugar

$1^1/_2$ tablespoons ground cinnamon

$^1/_2$ cup melted butter

White Fondant Glaze:

2 cups confectioners' sugar, sifted

$^1/_2$ teaspoon orange extract

$^1/_4$ cup warm milk

To make the sweet dough:

Cream together the sugar, salt, and shortening in the bowl of a food processor fitted with a dough blade until smooth—about 30 seconds. Add egg and lemon extract and pulse for 1 minute to combine. Add flour, yeast, and milk and pulse for 1 minute; then increase the speed and beat for about 6 minutes until the dough is silky and supple, tacky but not sticky. Add a little flour if your dough is too sticky. Lightly oil a large bowl with the vegetable oil. Transfer the sweet dough to the prepared bowl and toss it around to lightly coat the dough with oil. Cover the bowl with plastic wrap and place somewhere warm to rise until doubled in size, about 2 hours.

To make the cinnamon buns:

Lightly dust a clean, flat, and dry work surface with some of the flour. Transfer the proofed sweet dough to the lightly-dusted work surface. Lightly dust the rolling pin and the top of the sweet dough with more of the flour, and roll the dough out until it measures 14" x 12", and $^2/_3$-inch thick. Combine the sugar and cinnamon in a small bowl and stir with a spoon until well mixed. Sprinkle cinnamon sugar over the top of the dough. Roll the dough into a cigar shaped roll ending with the seam side facing down. Use a sharp knife to cut about 8–10 $1^3/_4$-inch pieces. Line a baking sheet with parchment paper. Place the buns spiral side up about $^1/_2$-inch apart on the parchment paper lined tray. Cover the buns with a towel and place somewhere warm to rise until doubled in size—about $1^1/_2$ hours.

Preheat the oven to 350°.

Bake the cinnamon buns on the center rack of the preheated oven until golden brown, about 25 minutes. Remove the buns from the oven and cool on the pan for 10 minutes. Make the white fondant glaze while the buns cool.

To make the fondant glaze:

Combine the confectioners' sugar and the orange extract in a medium bowl with a spoon. Slowly add the warm milk while constantly stirring until smooth. Drizzle this glaze over the cooling buns. Transfer the buns to a cooling rack for 20 minutes before serving.

✳ **CHEF'S NOTE:** You can make smaller cinnamon buns by rolling the dough 19 inches long and 9 inches wide, then into a long, cigar shape. Cut the smaller buns into $1^{1}/_{4}$-inch pieces instead of the $1^{3}/_{4}$-inch size for the larger buns.

8-10 SERVINGS

⊹ FOCACCIA

Focaccia is one of the jewels of Northern Italian cuisine. There are many toppings that would be fantastic to bake onto your focaccia. The type of topping you use will determine when you place it on the bread. Or, enjoy it simply finished with herb oil.

Herb Oil:
^{1}/$_2$ cup olive oil

1 tablespoon chopped parsley

1 tablespoon chopped basil

1 tablespoon chopped thyme

1 tablespoon chopped oregano

1 tablespoon kosher salt

2 teaspoons chopped garlic

1 teaspoon cracked black pepper

1 teaspoon paprika

1 teaspoon onion powder

1 teaspoon fennel seeds

^{1}/$_2$ teaspoon cayenne pepper

Focaccia Dough:
5^2/$_3$ cups unbleached bread flour

2 teaspoons salt

2 teaspoons instant yeast

2^1/$_4$ cups cold water

6^1/$_2$ tablespoons olive oil

To make the herb oil:
Combine all of the ingredients in a medium bowl and mix vigorously with a wire whisk. Set aside at room temperature until needed.

To make the focaccia:
Combine all the ingredients except the oil in a food processor fitted with a dough blade. Pulse for 1 minute; then switch the processor to allow the dough to mix for 3 additional minutes. Add 4 tablespoons of oil and continue to mix for an additional minute. Allow the dough to rest for 15 minutes; then pulse for 3 minutes. Coat the inside of a medium bowl with ^{1}/$_2$ tablespoon of olive oil. Transfer the dough to the prepared bowl, toss the dough in the bowl to coat with oil and cover with plastic wrap and refrigerate overnight until doubled in size.

To bake the focaccia:
Preheat the oven to 500°

Line a baking sheet with sides with parchment paper. Coat the parchment lined pan with the remaining 2 tablespoons of olive oil. Gently transfer the dough from the bowl to the prepared pan, trying not to de-gas the dough as best you can. Pour herb oil over the top of the dough and use you fingers to dimple the dough as you gently stretch it out on the pan. Let the dough rise until the pan is full of dough and it is puffy—about 2^1/$_2$ hours.

Place the focaccia on the center rack of the preheated oven and close the door. Reduce the temperature to 450° and bake until both the top and underside are golden and slightly crisp—about 20 minutes. Rotate the tray 180 degrees halfway through the baking time. Remove the focaccia from the oven and immediately transfer it to a cooling rack with a baking sheet underneath to catch any excess oil. Cool at room temperature for at least 20 minutes before serving.

✳ **CHEF'S NOTE:** Top with marinated sun-dried tomatoes, olives, roasted garlic, herbs, nuts, sautéed mushrooms, sautéed peppers, or sautéed onions before you proof the dough on the pan. Items such as high moisture cheeses (blue or feta), cooked meats, various pestos (parsley, spinach, roasted red pepper, or sun-dried tomato), or salt, should be placed on top of the dough just before you bake the focaccia. Dry cheeses such as Parmesan, grated mozzarella, grated cheddar, or grated Swiss should all be sprinkled on top about halfway through baking.

1 HALF SHEET TRAY

→ WALNUT AND LEMON TEA BREAD

A simple and delicious way to impress your guests at tea time or anytime! Quick and easy to prepare, the lemon glaze gives this bread extra flavor.

Walnut and Lemon Tea Bread:

4 ounces (1 stick), unsalted butter, cut into 1/2-ounce pieces, plus 2 teaspoons melted

3/4 cup granulated sugar

1/4 cup (2 ounces) tightly-packed light brown sugar

3 large eggs

1/2 teaspoon lemon extract

1 teaspoon vanilla extract

3/4 cup buttermilk

2 cups all-purpose flour

1 teaspoon baking powder

1/2 teaspoon baking soda

1/4 teaspoon salt

1/8 teaspoon ground cloves

1/8 teaspoon ground cinnamon

1/2 cup chopped toasted walnuts

Lemon Glaze:

1 1/2 cups powdered confectioners' sugar

1/4 cup fresh squeezed lemon juice

To make the bread:

Preheat the oven to 350°.

Lightly brush a nonstick loaf pan with some of the melted butter. Line the bottom of the pan with parchment paper or wax paper and set aside.

Place the remaining 4 ounces of butter and both sugars in the bowl of a food processor fitted with a metal or plastic blade. Beat on high speed for 4 minutes until soft. Add eggs one at a time allowing each to mix in completely before adding the next. Stop and scrape down the inside of the bowl. Add both of the extracts and the buttermilk, and mix to combine—about 3 minutes. Scrape down the bowl. Sift the remaining dry ingredients into a large bowl. Add walnuts, pour the egg mixture into the sifted dry ingredients, and fold together with a rubber spatula just until incorporated. Transfer this batter to the prepared loaf pan. Bake on the center rack of the preheated oven until a toothpick inserted into the center of the cake comes out clean—about 1 hour. Remove the cake from the oven and allow to cool in the pan at room temperature for 10 minutes. Turn the cake out onto a serving plate and refrigerate until cold—about 30 minutes.

To make the lemon glaze:

Sift the confectioners' sugar into a medium bowl. Add lemon juice and stir with a wooden spoon until well combined and smooth.

Spread this glaze over the top of the walnut and lemon tea bread.

✹ **CHEF'S NOTE:** If you want to serve this cake warm, allow it to cool slightly at room temperature while you prepare the glaze. If your glaze seems too tight, simply add a bit more lemon juice. On the other hand, if the glaze comes out too runny, add a small amount of sifted confectioners' sugar to thicken it.

8 SERVINGS

✣ MARBLE RYE BREAD

This delicious braided loaf will serve as the perfect accompaniment to a simple salad or pasta dish, and even make the simplest of sandwiches a hearty meal.

3 cups unbleached bread flour

1 1/3 cups white rye flour

1 1/3 teaspoons salt

1 1/2 cup water

1 3/4 teaspoons instant yeast

1 1/2 teaspoons caraway seeds

1 tablespoon molasses

2 tablespoons shortening

2 teaspoons vegetable oil

4 tablespoons unsweetened cocoa powder

1 large egg, lightly beaten

To make the marble rye:

Sift the 2 flours and salt into the bowl of a food processor fitted with a dough blade. Combine the water and yeast, and stir with a spoon until dissolved. Add this mixture to the sifted flours and salt. Pulse until they begin to blend—about 30 seconds. Add caraway seeds, molasses, and shortening. Turn the processor on and allow to mix until the dough forms one solid mass—about 3 minutes. Allow the dough to rest for 15 minutes; then mix again for 3 additional minutes. Lightly oil 2 medium bowls with vegetable oil. Transfer half of the dough to one of the prepared bowls and cover with a towel. Add cocoa powder to the other half of the dough in the processor and mix until incorporated—about 2 minutes. Transfer this dark dough to the other prepared bowl, cover it with a towel and place both bowls of dough somewhere warm to rise until doubled in size—about 2 hours.

Use your hands to punch each of the dough balls down to its original size. Cover them again with the towels and allow them to rise again to twice their size—about 2 additional hours.

Preheat the oven to 350°.

Transfer the balls of dough to a clean, dry, and flat work surface and punch the raised doughs down again. Use your hands to roll each into long cylinder shapes. Twist or braid the doughs together. Place the braided loaf on a baking sheet lined with parchment paper. Cover the loaf with a cloth and proof again until the loaf is double in size. Lightly brush the loaf with egg wash. Bake on the center rack of the preheated oven until golden brown and firm when tapped—about 35 minutes. Rotate the bread 180 degrees halfway through the baking time.

Remove from the oven and allow the bread to cool for at least 1 hour at room temperature.

✳ **CHEF'S NOTE:** A great place to proof dough (raise it) is in a gas oven with ONLY the pilot light on.

1 LARGE LOAF

⇢ GOURMET CHEESECAKE POPS

"Gourmet Pops are the latest addition to renowned Chef David Burke's line of imaginative gourmet appetizers". These innovative cheesecake pops will add a deliciously whimsical touch to your dessert platter and lend themselves to both last minute get-togethers and sophisticated formal events.

Cheesecake Pops:

2 teaspoons unsalted butter, melted

2 tablespoons all-purpose flour

$^1/_2$ pound cream cheese

5 tablespoons granulated sugar

1 tablespoon lemon zest

$^1/_8$ teaspoon kosher salt

6 tablespoons sour cream

3 large eggs

4 tablespoons whole milk

4 tablespoons heavy cream

8 ounces semisweet chocolate, coarsely chopped and melted

8 ounces milk chocolate, coarsely chopped and melted

8 ounces white chocolate, coarsely chopped and melted

$1^1/_2$ cups grated coconut, lightly toasted

1 cup mini chocolate chips

1 cup mini Reese's Pieces

To make the cheesecake pops:
Preheat the oven to 325°.

Lightly brush the insides of an 8-inch nonstick cake pan with melted butter. Dust the inside of the buttered pan with flour, being sure to coat the entire interior. Tap off any excess. Set aside.

Combine cream cheese and granulated sugar in the bowl of a food processor fitted with a metal blade. Pulse for 30 seconds. Increase the speed on the processor and cream until smooth—about 2 minutes. Add lime zest, salt, and sour cream.

Continue to cream for an additional minute. Add the eggs, one at a time allowing them to mix for 30 seconds after each addition. Scrape down the insides of the bowl with a rubber spatula. Add milk and cream, and pulse just to combine. Transfer this batter into the prepared pan and bake in a water bath on the center rack of the preheated oven for 1 hour. Reduce the heat to 300° and bake until a skewer inserted into the center of the cake comes out clean —about 30 minutes. Remove the cheesecake from the oven and cool at room temperature for 30 minutes in the pan. Remove the cheesecake from the pan and refrigerate until cold.

Using a small ice-cream scoop, make 40 cheesecake balls. Form the balls into smooth orbs and insert a lollypop stick into the center of each. Place the pops in the freezer for 45 minutes – 1 hour. Remove the frozen pops from the freezer and begin dipping them into the melted chocolates, being sure to coat the entire outside. Immediately coat the chocolate covered pops in your choice of coconut, mini chips, Reese's Pieces, or chopped nuts. Place in the refrigerator until ready for serving.

Serve the cheesecake pops on a large tray. A light dusting of powdered sugar over the entire tray would provide just the right accent and set the whole tray off.

✳ **CHEF'S NOTE:** Be creative and use any combination of chopped candy to garnish the outside of the chocolate-covered cheesecake pops.

40 CHEESECAKE POPS

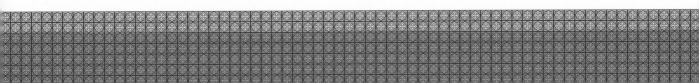

✦ CINNAMON STREUSEL SURPRISE

Taken from Chef Rose Levy Beranbaum's "The Bread Bible", this golden loaf, topped with fragrant cinnamon crumb, has a hidden tart layer of buttery apple slices nestled inside an extra layer of crumb. Perfect with coffee or tea, the Chef also recommends enjoying it with a glass of cold milk.

Crumb Topping and Filling:

1/4 cup tightly packed light brown sugar

1 1/2 tablespoons granulated sugar

3/4 cup walnuts, toasted

1 teaspoon cinnamon

1/4 cup plus 2 tablespoons cake flour, unsifted

3 tablespoons unsalted butter, melted

1/4 teaspoon vanilla extract

1 small Granny Smith apple (about 5 ounces)

Yogurt Batter:

1 large egg

2 large egg yolks

1/2 cup whole milk yogurt

1 teaspoon pure vanilla extract

1 1/2 cups sifted cake flour

3/4 cup granulated sugar

1/4 teaspoon baking powder

3/8 teaspoon baking soda

Scant 1/4 teaspoon salt

9 tablespoons unsalted butter, softened

To make the cinnamon crumb surprise:

Lightly spray the inside of a 9" x 5" nonstick loaf pan with Baker's Day®. Lightly dust the insides with all-purpose flour and tap out any excess. Set aside until needed.

Preheat the oven to 350°.

Place both sugars, walnuts, and cinnamon in the bowl of a food processor fitted with the metal blade. Pulse until the nuts are coarsely chopped — about 45 second. Transfer 1/2 cup of this mixture to a small bowl, and set aside. This will be used in the filling. Add flour, butter, and vanilla to the food processor and pulse for about 15 seconds to form a coarse, crumbly mixture for the topping. Transfer to small bowl and set aside.

Combine egg, egg yolks, 1/4 cup of yogurt, and vanilla in a medium bowl. Set aside. Place the cake flour, sugar, baking powder, baking soda, and salt in the bowl of a food processor fitted with a dough blade. Pulse for 30 seconds to combine. Add butter and the remaining yogurt, and pulse until the dry ingredients are moistened—about 1 minute. Process the mixture now for 1 minute. Scrape down the sides of the bowl with a rubber spatula. While pulsing, gradually add the egg mixture in 2 batches, pulsing for 20 seconds after each addition. Scrape down the sides and pulse for an additional 10 seconds.

Use a sharp paring knife, peel, core and quarter the apple. Slice each quarter into 1/4-inch slices lengthwise and set aside. Quickly pour about 2/3 of the batter into the prepared pan and smooth the surface with a spatula. Sprinkle the top with the 1/2 cup of crumb filling and working from the one end to the other, top with apple slices in 2 overlapping rows. Drop the remaining 1/3 of the batter over the apples and spread it evenly. Sprinkle with the remaining crumb topping. Bake on the center rack of the preheated oven until a wooden toothpick inserted in the center comes out clean—about 55

minutes. It may be necessary to loosely tent with buttered foil after 45 minutes to prevent over browning.

Remove from the oven and set the pan on a wire rack to cool for 10 minutes. Place a folded kitchen towel on top of a flat plate and cover it with plastic wrap. Lightly oil the plastic wrap. Loosen the sides of the loaf with a small metal spatula, and invert it onto the prepared plate. Grease a wire rack and re-invert the loaf onto it so the top faces up. Cool completely before wrapping airtight, about 1¹/₂ hours.

✷ CHEF'S NOTE: For a slightly firmer texture, you may use all-purpose flour, but it is imperative that it be bleached or the butter is likely to drop to the bottom, forming an unpleasant tasting and rubbery layer.

6 SERVINGS

⇾ DENSE CHOCOLATE CAKE

This cake would impress even if served with a simple syrup brushed on the outside. For a little extra "wow" you may consider a ganache and a topping of fresh raspberries.

³/₄ pound (3 sticks) unsalted butter cut into ¹/₂ ounce pieces, plus 2 teaspoons melted

7 ounces unsweetened chocolate, coarsely chopped

3 ounces bittersweet chocolate, coarsely chopped

¹/₄ cup heavy cream

1 tablespoon instant espresso powder

2 cups granulated sugar

3¹/₃-cups cake flour

1¹/₂ teaspoons baking soda

1 teaspoon salt

¹/₂ cup coffee liquor

1¹/₂ teaspoons pure vanilla extract

3 large eggs

To bake the dense chocolate cake:

Preheat the oven to 325∞ F.

Lightly brush the inside of a 9-inch nonstick cake pan with ¹/₄ the melted butter. Line the pan with parchment paper and lightly brush again with the remaining melted butter. Set aside.

Place the ³/₄ pound of butter, both chocolates, heavy cream, and espresso powder in the top half of a double boiler. Melt these ingredients over medium heat, stirring frequently with a rubber spatula until smooth — about 7 minutes. Add sugar to the melted chocolate mixture and whisk until dissolved. Allow to cool for 10 minutes.

Combine the flour baking soda and salt in a sifter. Sift these dry ingredients onto a large piece of parchment paper and set aside.

Transfer the chocolate-sugar mixture to the bowl of a food processor fitted with a metal blade. Add coffee liquor and vanilla extract. Increase the speed on the processor and beat for 2 minutes. Add eggs and continue to mix for an additional minute until well incorporated. Add the sifted dry ingredients and pulse until combined. Scrape down the inside of the processor bowl with a rubber spatula. Continue to mix the batter for 1 minute, until well combined. Transfer the batter to the prepared pan and smooth to the edges. Bake on the center rack of the preheated oven until a toothpick inserted into the center of the cake comes out clean—about 1¹/₂ hours.

Remove from the oven and allow to cool at room temperature in the pan for 10 minutes. Invert the cake pan onto a cake plate. Remove and discard the parchment paper on the bottom of the cake. Allow to cool for 30 minutes before serving.

✷ **CHEF'S NOTE:** You may substitute semisweet chocolate for bittersweet chocolate in this recipe.

8 – 12 SERVINGS

⚹ CROWNED APPLE CAKE

This recipe was originally made famous by Marlene Sorosky. As it bakes, the pure and natural ingredients will fill your kitchen with a delicious aroma. The pecan halves on top of the cake will toast as the cake bakes. You could substitute the walnuts for pecans if you like.

2 teaspoons unsalted butter, melted

4 large Granny Smith apples (about 2½ pounds)

⅓ cup clover honey

1 tablespoon ground cinnamon

3 cups all purpose flour

2 cups granulated sugar

1 cup vegetable oil

4 large eggs

⅓ cup orange juice

3 tablespoons baking powder

2½ teaspoon pure vanilla extract

1 teaspoon salt

*1 cup pecan halves, ½ of them cup toasted
and coarsely chopped*

To bake the cake:

Preheat the oven to 350°.

Lightly brush the inside of a nonstick tube pan with the melted butter. Set aside.

Peel, quarter, remove the core, and slice the apples lengthwise into ¼ inch thick slices. Place in a medium bowl; then add the honey and cinnamon, and toss to coat the apples so they don't oxidize.

Combine flour, sugar, oil, eggs, orange juice, baking powder, vanilla, and salt in the bowl of a food processor fitted with a beating blade. Operate the food processor on pulse for 1 minute until the mixture begins to combine. Increase the speed and allow the mixture to beat until well blended—about 2 minutes. Pour about 1/3 of the batter into the pan and spread evenly with a rubber spatula. Artfully arrange 1/3 of the apple slices on top of the batter; then sprinkle with the chopped pecans. Pour in about half of the remaining batter and spread evenly with a rubber spatula. Once again, artfully arrange half of the remaining apple slices on top of the batter. Top with the remaining batter, once again smoothing the top with a rubber spatula. Arrange the remaining apple slices over the top overlapping them in a pinwheel pattern. Pour any juices in the bowl left over from the honey, cinnamon, and apple slices over the top of the cake. Artfully arrange the pecan halves around the top of the cake. Place on a baking sheet with sides and bake on the center rack of the preheated oven for 85 minutes, or until a toothpick inserted into the center of the cake comes out clean.

Remove from the oven and allow it to cool in the pan at room temperature for 10 minutes. Loosen the cake from the pan by gently running a sharp knife around the outer edge. Turn the cake out onto a cake plate and set aside at room temperature until cool—about 2 hours.

✳ **CHEF'S NOTE:** Heat the honey in the microwave for 30 seconds so it is fluid enough to pour and coat the apple slices.

12 SERVINGS

⤏ YEAST-RAISED DOUGHNUTS

These decadent treats are simple to make at home, and will be sure to put smiles on the faces of children and adults alike. Encourage the entire family to be involved in the decoration of the doughnuts, and the selection of the various toppings.

3¹/₂ cups all-purpose flour

2 .25-ounce packages active dry yeast

³/₄ cup whole milk

³/₄ cup granulated sugar

2 ounces unsalted butter, cut into ¹/₂-ounce pieces

¹/₂ teaspoon salt

2 large eggs

2 quarts vegetable oil

1 cup confectioners' sugar for dusting

To make the doughnuts:

Combine 1³/₄ cups of flour with the yeast in the bowl of a food processor fitted with a dough blade. Heat milk, sugar, butter, and salt in a medium saucepan over medium heat. Dissolve the sugar and continue stirring until the butter has melted. Pour this hot milk mixture into the bowl of the food processor with the flour and yeast. Operate the processor on pulse for 1 minute. Add eggs and continue to pulse for 30 seconds. Scrape down the inside of the processor bowl with a rubber spatula. Increase the speed on the processor and beat the dough until it becomes smooth and supple—about 2 minutes. Lightly coat the inside of a medium bowl with 2 teaspoons of vegetable oil. Transfer the dough to the oiled bowl. Cover with a towel and let the dough rise in a warm location until it doubles in size—about 1 hour.

Generously dust a flat, dry work surface with some of the remaining flour. Turn raised dough out onto the floured surface. Use your fingers, punch down the dough; then dust a rolling pin and the top of the dough with more flour and roll the dough out to 1¹/₂-inch thickness. Cut out doughnuts with a floured doughnut cutter. Re-roll trimmings and cut them into doughnuts as well. Transfer doughnuts to parchment paper-lined baking sheets. Cover with towels and let rise 45 minutes, until they have doubled in size.

Heat the remaining oil in a deep-fryer or a large, heavy-gauge stock pot to 360°. Fry doughnuts, in batches, turning several times, until golden all over — about 5 minutes each. Using a slotted spoon remove doughnuts to a rack to drain. Allow the doughnuts to cool at room temperature for 20 minutes. Use a mesh strainer to dust the doughnuts with confectioners' sugar. Serve immediately.

✳ **CHEF'S NOTE:** If you cannot locate a doughnut cutter, simply use large and small circle cutters.

1 ¹/₂ DOZEN DOUGHNUTS

→ FLAKY ALMOND FRUIT TART

This dessert is a real treat for fruit and nut lovers. Regular almonds can be used in place of almond paste in this recipe, and you can substitute other seasonal fruit for the berries. Make a tropical theme if that's what you prefer!

1 box frozen puff pastry

$^1/_2$ pound almond paste

2 large eggs

1 large egg yolk

4 ounces unsalted butter (1 stick), cut into $^1/_2$ ounce pieces

1 tablespoon cake flour

12 large strawberries, washed, patted dry and, green top trimmed off

$^1/_2$ pint raspberries

$^1/_2$ pint blueberries, washed, and patted dry

1 kiwi fruit peeled and sliced thin

$^1/_2$ cup apricot preserves

To bake the tart:

Preheat the oven to 325°

Remove the puff pastry from the box and unroll the sheet onto a clean, dry, and flat work surface. Place a 10-inch plate on top of the dough. Use a sharp knife to cut around the plate. Roll up any unused dough, and return it to the freezer. Remove the plate and transfer the dough circle to a baking sheet lined with parchment paper. Set aside at room temperature.

Combine the almond paste, eggs, egg yolk, unsalted butter, and cake flour in the bowl of a food processor fitted with a dough blade. Pulse the mixture for 30 seconds. With the processor running continously allow this mixture to beat for 2 minutes until well combined. Transfer this mixture, known as frangipane, to a pastry bag fitted with a large straight tip. Pipe the frangipane onto the circle of puff pastry in a circular motion starting in the center and working your way to the edge leaving $^1/_4$ inch of the puff pastry edge showing. Bake on the center rack of the preheated oven until firm and golden brown, about—20 minutes.

Remove the tart from the oven and cool at room temperature for 30 minutes.

Artfully arrange the fruit on the top of the tart. Heat a small nonstick sauté pan over medium heat. When hot, add apricot preserves and stir until smooth and fluid—about 1$^1/_2$ minutes. Brush apricot preserves over the top of the fruit on the tart making it glisten. Serve the tart immediately or refrigerate until ready to serve.

✳ **CHEF'S NOTE:** You may be able to purchase frangipane at a specialty grocery or from your local bakery if time is an issue. Or if you are unable to locate almond paste.

6 SERVINGS

✣ PEAR TART WITH ALMOND CREAM

Chef Rose Levy Beranbaum suggests the pears become more flavorful if allowed to sit in the poaching syrup for at least 24 hours. The recipe for this tart can be found in her book, "The Pie and Pastry Bible".

1 pre-baked pie crust

Pear filling:

*3 large ripe Bartlett pears (about 1³/4 pounds), plus
  1 seckle or other very small pear*

2¹/4 cups water

1 tablespoon freshly squeezed lemon juice

3 tablespoons kirsch

¹/4 cup plus 2 tablespoons granulated sugar

*¹/2 fresh vanilla bean about 1¹/2 inches, split in half
  lengthwise*

Almond Cream:

1 cup sliced blanched almonds

¹/2 cup granulated sugar

2 tablespoons bleached all-purpose flour

3¹/2 ounces unsalted butter, softened

2 large eggs, at room temperature

¹/2 teaspoon pure vanilla extract

Pear Glaze:

³/4 cup reserved syrup from poaching pears

³/4 teaspoon cornstarch

To pre-bake the pie crust:

On a pastry cloth rubbed with flour or, between two sheets of plastic wrap, roll the dough out using more flour as needed until it reaches 13 inches in diameter, and about ¹/8-inch thick. Line pan, turning excess down and pushing the sides so that they are about ¹/8-inch above the sides of the pan. Cover with plastic wrap and freeze for at least 30 minutes or refrigerate for at least 3 hours.

Preheat the oven to 425°.

Line the dough in the pan with parchment paper, pleating it as necessary to fit the shape of the pan, or simply use a large cup-shaped coffee filter. Fill the filter with dried beans, making sure the beans are pushed up well against sides of the filter. Bake on the center rack of the preheated oven for 20 minutes. Lift out the beans and prick all over with a fork (only halfway through if there will be a sticky or runny filling). Return the dough to the oven without the beans to bake for an additional 5–10 minutes or until pale golden brown. Check after 3 minutes, it may be necessary to prick the crust again if the upper layer of dough bubbles up. Remove the pre-baked crust from the oven and set aside at room temperature until needed.

To make the pear filling:

Quickly peel the pears, cut them in half lengthwise and remove the cores with a Parisian scoop. Heat water, lemon juice, kirsch, sugar, and vanilla bean in a large sauté pan over medium-high heat. Stir to dissolve the sugar. Place the pears in a single layer in the pan, top with a piece of parchment and bring to a boil. Reduce the heat to low. Place a lid on the pan and simmer until the pears are tender, but slightly firm—about 9 minutes. Remove the pan from the heat, slightly crack the lid on the pan and cool at room temperature for 1 hour. Transfer the pears and their liquid to a bowl small enough so the pears are covered with liquid. Cover it tightly and refrigerate until ready to use.

To make the almond cream:

Place almonds, sugar, and flour in a food processor fitted with the metal blade. Process until the almonds are very fine — about 1 minute. Transfer all but $1/2$ cup of the almond-flour mixture to a small bowl and set aside. Add soft butter and continue processing until combined. Add one egg along with another $1/2$ cup of the almond-flour mixture and process until combined; then process in the second egg along with the remaining mixture until thoroughly incorporated. Add vanilla and pulse for 10 seconds. Transfer the almond cream to a medium bowl and refrigerate for 10 minutes before assembling the tart.

To bake the tart:

Preheat oven to 350°

Spread chilled almond cream evenly into the baked, cooled tart shell. Set aside.

Drain pears well on paper towels, rounded sides up, reserving poaching liquid and vanilla beans. Using a sharp, thin-bladed knife, slice each pear widthwise into thin slices, but do not slice all the way through to the bottom. Press gently on top of each pear to fan the slices slightly. Position each fanned out pear on top of the almond cream, pointed ends facing in and meeting at the center. Set the small pear in the center. Bake on the center rack of the preheated oven until the almond cream puffs slightly, surrounding the pears, and turns golden brown—about 30 minutes. When pressed very lightly with a fingertip, the almond cream will spring back. Remove tart from the oven and cool in the pan on a wire rack while making the glaze.

To make the glaze and finish the tart:

Scrape the insides of the reserved vanilla bean out, and transfer them to a small saucepan. Add $3/4$ cup of reserved poaching liquid, and bring to a boil over medium-high heat. Reduce the heat to a simmer and cook until the liquid is quite thick and is reduced to about $1/4$ cup. Add cornstarch, and stir to dissolve. Allow to simmer for an additional 20 seconds until very thick and transparent. Remove glaze from the heat and pour immediately into a small cup. Use a pastry brush to coat the pears well with glaze. Brush any remaining glaze onto the nut filling. Use a sharp knife to cut the tart into 6 equally-sized pieces and serve.

✳ **CHEF'S NOTE:** The parchment keeps the tops of the pears moistened while cooling and prevents discoloration. The finished tart may be stored at room temperature if being eaten the same day, or refrigerated for up to 3 days. It is preferable to allow it to come to room temperature before serving. The almond cream may be refrigerated for 1 week or frozen for 1 month.

6 SERVINGS

✦ INDEX

→ ABOUT THE UNIVERSITY AND "MASTER CLASS AT JOHNSON & WALES"

Johnson & Wales—America's Career University®— was founded in 1914. It is a private, non-profit accredited institution offering undergraduate and graduate degree programs in business, food service, hospitality and technology. With an enrollment of more than 15,000 students, Johnson & Wales is based in Providence, R.I., and maintains campuses in Charleston, S.C.; Norfolk, Va.; North Miami, Fla; Denver, Colo.; and Göteborg, Sweden with plans to open a new campus in Charlotte, N.C. in 2004. For more information about Johnson & Wales University, visit www.jwu.edu

When Johnson & Wales first opened its doors in 1914, with "two students and one typewriter," its founders, Gertrude Johnson and Mary Wales never envisioned the Johnson & Wales University of today, with more than 15,000 students from all 50 states and over 90 countries studying at five domestic campuses. They had no idea that students would earn both undergraduate and graduate degrees broadened by educational partnerships around the globe. They could not have conceived that 59 years later the University would open a College of Culinary Arts dedicated to continuing its longstanding tradition of offering students hands-on training for important careers in critical segments of industry, or that it would become the world's largest food service educator.

Our focus, as America's Career University®, is always on our students and making their education relevant in today's job market. As we work toward the 2004 opening of a campus in Charlotte, N.C., we are particularly excited about consolidating our presence in the Southeast. Charlotte is a campus growing from the ground up, in partnership with the Charlotte community and in response to the needs of its business establishments. In state-of-the-art facilities we will offer our distinct brand of education in another region of the nation, working with employers to ensure that our graduates are equipped with real-world skills aligned with industry needs. Whether through programs in culinary arts, hospitality, business or technology, it is our mission to prepare students for jobs that best fit their career goals, and to sustain that effort across all disciplines and all campuses.

What is taught to our students at each of our campus locations prepares them with an educational experience second to none. The success of our first efforts to offer food lovers around the country an opportunity to cook with our chefs and students through "Master Class at Johnson & Wales" on public television, and its companion cookbook, fueled our second series and this accompanying cookbook. While a true labor of love, it is yet another extension of our commitment to providing the highest quality educational experience, not only in our classrooms, labs and kitchens, but outside our campus locations as well.

JOHNSON & WALES
UNIVERSITY

America's Career University®

BIBLIOGRAPHY

Herbst, Sharon Tyler. *The New Food Lover's Companion.* 3rd ed.
    Hauppauge, New York: Barron's 2001
Riely, Elizabeth. *The Chef's Companion.* 2nd ed. John Wiley &
    Sons 1996

Cuisinart is proud to sponsor

Public Broadcasting's

"Master Class at Johnson & Wales".

When Cuisinart introduced home

cooks to the world-famous food

processor, we shared a secret

professional cooks had

known for years. Today, we

continue to strive for culinary

excellence, and this is why

we are pleased to be part of

"Master Class at Johnson & Wales".

SAVOR THE GOOD LIFE®

www.cuisinart.com

Cuisinart
SAVOR THE GOOD LIFE®

Cuisinart. Today our name is as familiar to those who exercise their culinary skills at home as it is to those who cook professionally. Ever since we introduced our legendary food processor in 1973, we've been committed to saving you time in the kitchen while continuing to open up a wide new range of creative cooking options. Today Cuisinart® products make time-consuming tasks seem effortless as delicious meals become easy with our products at your side. We include recipes with our appliances, to guide you every step of the way. Trust Cuisinart to make your time in the kitchen more rewarding... and much more fun!

Cuisinart® Premier Series Food Processors

The next generation Cuisinart food processor offers sleek, contemporary looks and more food prep options than ever! The Premier Series is smooth – all curves, with wipe-clean solid state touchpads. These new models feature a separate dough control that automatically adjusts the motor to the right speed for kneading, and a specially designed metal dough blade to make the process perfect. With one-piece, extra large feed tubes, dishwasher safe parts, and a variety of shredding and slicing discs, the Cuisinart® Food Processor – Premier Series or Classic – remains the ultimate food prep tool.

Smart Stick® Extendable Hand Blender

Leave it to Cuisinart to extend your blending options! Our Smart Stick® Extendable Shaft Hand Blender features an adjustable shaft that easily extends to reach deep into big pots of soup and sauces and into the very bottom of tall pitchers. Four speeds, plus our handy Mini-Prep® Chopper/Grinder, a whipping disc and a chopping blade, further extend your food prep options.

SmartPower CountUp® 9-Speed Electronic Hand Mixer

This is the mixer you can count on. Literally! A digital timer, built right into an exceptionally comfortable handle, starts running the instant you start mixing. You'll never over – or under – mix again. With 220 watts, automatic feedback power that kicks in when needed, 9 speeds (including 3 extra low and a really Smooth Start™), plus a chef's whisk, you'll find there's very little this mixer can't handle!

Cuisinart®
SAVOR THE GOOD LIFE®

Cuisinart® countertop appliances are designed to be versatile and easy to use. They reduce the time you spend on the mundane tasks of food preparation, allowing you the freedom to be a little more creative in the kitchen. Crafted from the finest quality materials, each product reflects Cuisinart's commitment to quality, innovation and performance. From our "one and only" original Food Processor, to our toasters, blenders, mixers and coffeemakers, Cuisinart® products stand ready to offer you years of service. Enjoy your time with us. We think you will find it absolutely delicious!

SmartPower Premier™ 600 Watt Blender

Cuisinart brings a new look and more power to blending. Industrial cast metal and smooth brushed stainless house a powerful 600-watt motor. This do-it-all Premier Blender will crush ice, breeze through heavy-duty blending tasks, or perfectly mince a handful of fresh herbs. The 50-ounce glass blender jar is big enough to double or triple your favorite recipes. A built-in Count-Up™ Timer tracks every second of blending time!

Metal Classic Toaster

Cuisinart's trendsetting new look in toasting. Brushed stainless housing is smoothed into elegant curves, making it a perfect fit in today's commercial-look kitchen. It includes Bagel, Reheat, and Defrost buttons with LED indicators, and a 6-setting custom Browning Dial. An Extra-Lift Carriage brings small items up higher for easy removal.

Grind & Brew Thermal™ Coffeemaker

Cuisinart presents a coffeemaker unparalleled in looks and performance! The streamlined, brushed stainless Grind & Brew Thermal™ automatically grinds whole beans just before brewing, for the freshest, most flavorful coffee. A unique airtight, brew-through/pour-through lid lets fresh, hot coffee brew right into the double-walled insulated stainless steel thermal carafe. Coffee lovers will appreciate the charcoal water filter and gold tone coffee filter, as well as separate, easy-to-clean grinding and filter chambers. This fully programmable coffeemaker delivers the sweetest wakeup call ever – the freshest, hot, just-brewed coffee!

Cuisinart®
SAVOR THE GOOD LIFE®

30 years ago, Cuisinart established a new standard in professional cookware. Today we offer three distinctive lines, each including a full range of basic and specialty pieces, to suit every style of cooking. Cuisinart uses only the finest professional quality materials in the construction of our cookware. Designed from the inside out for today's healthy, relaxed lifestyles, all three lines bring together versatile functionality and the pleasure of presentation. From stovetop to oven to tabletop, Cuisinart® Cookware makes cooking a pleasure.

Cuisinart® MultiClad Stainless Cookware

Cuisinart honors a 30+ year commitment to producing only top-quality, innovative cookware with the MultiClad Stainless Collection. The triple-ply construction combines the highest grade stainless steel and pure, solid

aluminum to create a line of cookware that perfectly performs all of the classic cooking techniques. The look is sensational. Smooth, brushed stainless steel exteriors. Mirror-finish, naturally stick-free stainless cooking surfaces. And sandwiched between, a pure aluminum core that extends across the bottoms and up the sides for unparalleled heat conduction. Tightfitting lids seal in flavor and nutrients for results that are consistently delicious.

Cuisinart® Stick Free Stainless Non-Stick Cookware

Cuisinart has combined nonstick convenience with professional quality cookware, setting a new standard in nonstick cookware.

The Stick Free Stainless line is designed for flavorful, healthful cooking. Through a special Excalibur® Multi-Layer System, stainless steel is actually built into the nonstick material for superior durability.

Chef's Classic™ Stainless Cookware

Cuisinart presents a dazzling line of highly polished 18/10 stainless steel cookware that looks spectacular hanging in any kitchen. Stainless steel delivers unsurpassed durability and performance, and an encapsulated base provides excellent heat retention and conduction. Solid, stainless steel riveted handles are joined to cookware in a unique open Y-shape to keep them cool on the stovetop. All Chef's Classic™ Stainless is dishwasher safe.

NOTES

NOTES